LOHENGRIN

Opera in Three Acts

by

Richard Wagner

English Version by
STEWART ROBB

Ed. 2541

G. SCHIRMER, *Inc.*

Important Notice

Performances of this opera must be licensed by the publisher.

All rights of any kind with respect to this opera and any parts thereof, including but not limited to stage, radio, television, motion picture, mechanical reproduction, translation, printing, and selling are strictly reserved.

License to perform this work, in whole or in part, whether with instrumental or keyboard accompaniment, must be secured in writing from the Publisher. Terms will be quoted upon request.

Copying of either separate parts or the whole of this work, by hand or by any other process, is unlawful and punishable under the provisions of the U.S.A. Copyright Act.

The use of any copies, including arrangements and orchestrations, other than those issued by the Publisher, is forbidden.

All inquiries should be directed to the Publisher:

G. Schirmer Rental Department
5 Bellvale Road
Chester, NY 10918
(914) 469-2271

45551c

LOHENGRIN

When Richard Wagner (1813-1883) was collecting the materials out of which he built *Tannhäuser,* he read the famous medieval poem *Der Wartburgkrieg.* This poem, narrating the story of a notable contest of song at the Wartburg Castle, dealt with Wolfram von Eschenbach as if he were a legendary personage. Wagner, knowing that he was a reality, procured his great epic, *Parzival,* and drew from it much of the material used in *Lohengrin.* It was while passing the summer of 1845 at Marienbad that Wagner laid out the plan of the work. He wrote the book in the course of the following winter and the music the next year.

Wagner began the composition of the music with the narrative of Lohengrin in the last scene of the third act, because, like Senta's ballad in *The Flying Dutchman,* that passage contained the musical germs of the whole work. The third act, then, was composed between September 9, 1846, and March 5, 1847, while he was at Grossgraufen, near Pillnitz. The first act was composed between May 12 and June 8, 1847. The second act was written between June 18 and August 2, 1847, and the prelude was completed on August 28 of the same year. The instrumentation occupied the composer during the following winter and spring. The score of the opera remained unpublished for some years, because Meser, who had brought out Wagner's previous works, had lost much money by them, and declined to touch *Lohengrin.* The rights of publication were subsequently acquired at a small price by Breitkopf & Härtel.

Managers were equally unwilling to risk the fortunes of a public production of a new work by a much-criticized and generally misunderstood master. Wagner tells us how he took out the score one day, and gazing at it, was filled with sorrow that the notes might never "sound from off the death-pale paper." In despair he wrote to Liszt, his good friend and the musical god of Weimar, begging him to perform the work, and back came the answer that it was already in preparation. Wagner himself did not hear *Lohengrin* till 1859, but it was produced at Weimar, Liszt conducting, on August 28, 1850.

Lohengrin had its first performance in New York in 1874—in Italian! At the Metropolitan, too, it was first performed in Italian during the season 1883-1884. When it was at last presented in the original language, the Metropolitan did so with a star cast, rarely if ever equaled in the history of the work. Lillian Nordica was the Elsa, Marie Brema the Ortrud, Jean de Reszke the Lohengrin, Kaschmann the Telramund, and Edouard de Reszke the King.

THE STORY

ACT I. King Henry the Fowler, visiting tenth-century Antwerp to raise an army, holds court under an oak tree on the banks fo the river Scheldt. He calls on the regent, Frederick of Telramund, to explain why the duchy of Brabant is torn by strife and disorder. Telramund accuses his ward, Elsa, sister to the vanished heir of Brabant, of murdering her brother; convinced of her guilt, he gave up his right to Elsa's hand and married Ortrud instead. Elsa is summoned to defend herself and describes the vision in which she has beheld a knight in shining armor, who will champion her cause and whom she will wed. Twice the herald calls on him to step forward, but only after Elsa has added her prayer does Lohengrin appear, drawn up the river in a boat by a swan, to which he bids a sad farewell. The knight, greeted by Elsa as her champion, betroths himself to her on condition that she shall never ask his name or whence he comes. If she does so, he must leave. On her assent, King Henry invokes divine guidance, whereupon Lohengrin proceeds to defeat Telramund in single combat and thus to establish Elsa's innocence. She falls joyously into her savior's arms and the pair are borne off in triumph.

ACT II. Huddling before dawn in the castle courtyard, the ambitious Ortrud spurs Telramund on to assail Lohengrin's power while she herself works on Elsa's curiosity. No sooner has Elsa appeared on the balcony and voiced her serenity to the breezes than Ortrud, appealing to pagan gods for help, attempts to sow distrust in the mind of the bride. In reply Elsa urges the unhappy woman to have faith and proffers friendship, which Ortrud resolves to turn to her own use. The two enter the castle as dawn breaks and the nobles assemble, eagerly anticipating the day's events. Telramund, banned as a traitor, furtively persuades four of his henchmen to side with him against Lohengrin, whom the herald proclaims Guardian of Brabant. The courtiers welcome Elsa as she and her bridal retinue enter in stately procession. At the steps of the cathedral, first Ortrud and then Telramund attempt to break up the wedding, she by suggesting that the unknown knight is an impostor and he by accusing Lohengrin of sorcery. The crowd stirs uneasily. Although Elsa assures her champion that she believes in him, the poison of doubt begins to work. King Henry leads the couple into church.

ACT III. After a brilliant orchestral introduction, the curtain rises on the bridal chamber, to which Elsa is escorted by her maidens in the well-known Wedding Chorus. The King leads in Lohengrin, gives his blessing to the pair and retires with the company. As their voices die away, the knight draws Elsa to him and joins her in a rapturous duet, which gives way to growing anxiety on the part of the bride, when in hysterical despair, she begs to know his name and whence he comes. Suddenly Telramund and the four treacherous nobles burst upon the scene. With a cry Elsa hands Lohengrin his sword, with which the knight strikes his enemy lifeless. Ordering the nobles to bear Telramund's body to the King, he sadly tells Elsa that he will meet her there and answer her questions.

Again on the banks of the Scheldt, King Henry holds assembly in preparation for marching against the foe. Telramund's bier is brought in, followed by Elsa, scarcely able to walk, and Lohengrin, who declares that he cannot lead them, reveals that he has slain the traitor in self-defense, and explains his parentage and the distant country to which he now must return. His home is the temple of the Holy Grail at Monsalvat; Parsifal is his father and Lohengrin his name. Prophesying victory for the King's forces, the knight sorrowfully bids Elsa farewell and turn to his faithful swan, which has meanwhile neared the shore. Ortrud rushes in, exulting in Elsa's betrayal of the one man who could have broken the evil spell that transformed into a swan her lost brother Gottfried. But as Lohengrin prays, a dove descends and hovers over the swan, which vanishes; Gottfried steps forth in its place. The dove draws the boat away with Lohengrin as Elsa expires in her brother's arms.

Courtesy of Opera News

CAST OF CHARACTERS

LOHENGRIN, Knight of the Holy Grail . . . . Tenor

HENRY I, King of Germany . . . . Bass

FREDERICK TELRAMUND, a Noble of Brabant . . . . Baritone

THE ROYAL HERALD . . . . Bass

GOTTFRIED, Elsa's brother . . . . Mute

FOUR NOBLES OF BRABANT . . . . Tenors and Basses

ELSA OF BRABANT . . . . Soprano

ORTRUD, wife of Telramund . . . . Mezzo-Soprano

FOUR PAGES . . . . Sopranos and Altos

Chorus of Saxon and Brabantian Nobles, Ladies, Pages, etc.

Antwerp, First Half of the 10th Century.

SYNOPSIS OF SCENES

LOHENGRIN

ERSTER AUFZUG

Eine Aue am Ufer der Schelde bei Antwerpen. König Heinrich. Friedrich von Telramund. Ortrud. Der Heerrufer. Sächsische und brabantische Grafen, Edle und Volk. Vier Heerhornbläser. Die Bläser blasen den Königsruf.

DER HEERRUFER

Hört! Grafen, Edle, Freie von Brabant!
Heinrich, der Deutschen König, kam zur Statt,
Mit euch zu dingen nach des Reiches Recht.
Gebt ihr nun Fried' und Folge dem Gebot?

DIE BRABANTER

Wir geben Fried' und Folge dem Gebot.
Willkommen! Willkommen, König, in Brabant!

KÖNIG HEINRICH

Gott grüss' euch, liebe Männer von Brabant!
Nicht müssig tat zu euch ich diese Fahrt;
Der Not des Reiches seid von mir gemahnt!
Soll ich euch erst der Drangsal Kunde sagen,
Die deutsches Land so oft aus Osten traf?
In fernster Mark heisst Weib und Kind ihr beten:
"Herr Gott, bewahr' uns vor der Ungarn Wut!"
Doch mir, des Reiches Haupt, musst' es geziemen,
So wilder Schmach ein Ende zu ersinnen;
Als Kampfes Preis gewann ich Frieden auf
Neun Jahr', ihn nützt' ich zu des Reiches Wehr:
Beschirmte Städt' und Burgen liess ich bau'n,
Den Heerbann übte ich zum Widerstand.

Zu End' ist nun die Frist, der Zins versagt,
Mit wildem Drohen rüstet sich der Feind.
Nun ist es Zeit, des Reiches Ehr' zu wahren;
Ob Ost, ob West, das gelte Allen gleich!
Was deutsches Land heisst, stelle Kampfesscharen,
Dann schmäht wohl niemand mehr das deutsche Reich.

DIE SACHSEN
(an die Waffen schlagend)
Wohlauf! Mit Gott für deutschen Reiches Ehr'!

KÖNIG
Komm' ich zu euch nun, Männer von Brabant,
Zum Heeresfolg' nach Mainz euch zu entbieten,
Wie muss mit Schmerz und Klagen ich erseh'n,
Dass ohne Fürsten ihr in Zwietracht lebt!
Verwirrung, wilde Fehde wird mir kund;
Drum ruf' ich dich, Friedrich von Telramund!
Ich kenne dich als aller Tugend Preis,
Jetzt rede, dass der Drangsal Grund ich weiss.

FRIEDRICH
Dank, König, dir, dass du zu richten kamst!
Die Wahrheit künd' ich, Untreu' ist mir fremd.
Zum Sterben kam der Herzog von Brabant,
Und meinem Schutz empfahl er seine Kinder,
Elsa, die Jungfrau, und Gottfried, den Knaben;
Mit Treue pflag ich seiner grossen Jugend,
Sein Leben war das Kleinod meiner Ehre.
Ermiss nun, König, meinen grimmen Schmerz,
Als meiner Ehre Kleinod mir geraubt!
Lustwandelnd führte Elsa den Knaben einst
Zum Wald, doch ohne ihn kehrte sie zurück;

1

LOHENGRIN

ACT ONE

A plain on the banks of the Scheldt, near Antwerp; the river winds towards the background, so that on the right a portion of it is hidden by trees. In the foreground, to the left, King Henry is seated under a sturdy oak; near him stand the Saxon and Thuringian nobles. On the other side are Frederick of Telramund and Ortrud. In the background, retainers. The Herald and four Trumpeters advance into an open circle. Trumpets sound.

HERALD

Hark! Princes, nobles, freemen of
   Brabant!
Henry, our German sovereign, has
   arrived
To hold a parley on our kingdom's
   rights.
Are you at one, and ready to obey?

BRABANTIANS

We are at one, and ready to obey!
Be welcome, be welcome, Sovereign, to
   Brabant.

KING HENRY

God greet you, loyal liegemen of
   Brabant!
The journey I have made was not for
   naught;
I come to warn of danger to the realm!
Need I relate to you the dire disasters
Which often from the East have swept
   our land?
How on our frontiers pray our wives
   and children:
"Lord God, protect us from Hungarian
   rage!"
Yet I, as kingdom's head, knew it my
   duty
To put an end to shame so wild and
   woeful;
As prize of war I won the peace
For full nine years, and used the time
   to arm the land.
I fortified the towns and raised up
   towers,
And now I summon you to take up
   arms.

The term is at an end, our tribute too.
Our foe prepares with wild and
   rumbling threats.
Now it is time to guard our nation's
   honor;
From East, from West, need do we
   have of all!
Rouse up the warriors throughout all
   the country,
Then no one evermore will shame our
   land!

THE SAXONS *(clashing their arms)*

With God we'll guard the honor of our
   land!

THE KING

Men of Brabant, I've come to you this
   day
To summon you to Mentz, with all your
   forces.
Great are my pain and woe to see you
   thus,
Dwelling in discord since you lack a
   lord.
Confusion, furious feuding meet me
   here.
So let me hear, Frederick of
   Telramund!
I know you as a man of mighty worth,
Now tell me what it is that brought
   this strife.

FREDERICK

Thanks, noble king, for having come
   to judge!
The truth is open, falsehood is my foe!
When death approached our great duke
   of Brabant,
He chose to make me guardian of his
   children,
Elsa, the maiden, and Gottfried, her
   brother.
I nursed his growing youth with stead-
   fast conscience.
His life was as the jewel of my honor.
Conceive now, sovereign, of my
   grievous pain,
When of this selfsame jewel I am
   robbed!
Elsa one day with Gottfried went
   rambling
In the woods, and yet she came back
   without the boy.

1

Mit falscher Sorge frug sie nach dem
  Bruder,
Da sie, von ungefähr von ihm verirrt,
Bald seine Spur, so sprach sie, nicht
  mehr fand.
Fruchtlos war all' Bemüh'n um den
  Verlor'nen;
Als ich mit Drohen nun in Elsa drang,
Da liess in bleichem Zagen und
  Erbeben
Der grässlichen Schuld Bekenntnis sie
  uns seh'n.
Es fasste mich Entsetzen vor der Magd;
Dem Recht auf ihre Hand, vom Vater
  mir
Verlieh'n, entsagt' ich willig da und
  gern,
Und nahm ein Weib, das meinem Sinn
  gefiel:
Ortrud, Radbod's, des Friesenfürsten,
  Spross.
Nun führ' ich Klage wider Elsa von
Brabant: des Brudermordes zeih' ich
  sie.
Dies Land doch sprech' ich für mich an
  mit Recht,
Da ich der Nächste von des Herzogs
  Blut,
Mein Weib dazu aus dem Geschlecht,
  das einst
Auch diesen Landen seine Fürsten gab.
Du hörst die Klage, König! Richte
  recht!

ALLE MÄNNER

Ha, schwerer Schuld zeiht Telramund!
Mit Grau'n werd' ich der Klage kund.

KÖNIG

Welch' fürchterliche Klage sprichst du
  aus!
Wie wäre möglich solche grosse
  Schuld?

FRIEDRICH

O Herr, traumselig ist die eitle Magd,
Die meine Hand voll Hochmut von sich
  stiess.
Geheimer Buhlschaft klag' ich sie drum
  an:
Sie wähnte wohl, wenn sie des Bruders
  ledig,
Dann könnte sie als Herrin von
  Brabant
Mit Recht dem Lehnsmann ihre Hand
  verwehren,
Und offen des geheimen Buhlen
  pflegen.

KÖNIG

Ruft die Beklagte her! Beginnen soll
Nun das Gericht! Gott lass' mich weise
  sein!

DER HEERRUFER

Soll hier nach Recht und Macht
  Gericht gehalten sein?

KÖNIG

Nicht eh'r soll bergen mich der
  Schild,
Bis ich gerichtet streng und mild!

ALLE MÄNNER

Nicht ch'r zur Scheide kehr' das
  Schwert,
Bis ihm durch Urteil Recht gewährt!

HEERRUFER

Wo ihr des Königs Schild gewahrt,
Dort Recht durch Urteil nun erfahrt!
Drum ruf' ich klagend laut und hell:
Elsa, erscheine hier zur Stell'!

(Elsa tritt auf; sie verweilt eine Zeit
  lang im Hintergrund; dann schreitet
  sie sehr langsam dem Vorgrund zu.
  Frauen folgen ihr, bleiben aber zu-
  nächst im Hintergrund an der äusser-
  sten Grenze des Gerichtskreises.)

DIE MÄNNER

Seht hin! Sie naht, die hart Beklagte!
Ha, wie erscheint sie so licht und
  rein!
Der sie so schwer zu zeihen wagte,
Wie sicher muss der Schuld er sein.

KÖNIG

Bist du es, Elsa von Brabant?
  (Elsa neigt das Haupt bejahend.)
Erkennst du mich als deinen Richter
  an?
(Elsa wendet ihr Haupt nach dem
  König, blickt ihm in's Auge und be-
  jaht dann mit vertrauensvoller Ge-
  bärde.)
So frage ich weiter: ist die Klage dir
  bekannt,
Die schwer hier wider dich erhoben?
(Elsa erblick Friedrich und Ortrud,
  neigt traurig das Haupt und bejaht.)
Was entgegnest du der Klage?
(Elsa—durch eine Gebärde: "nichts")
So bekennst du deine Schuld?
(Elsa blickt eine zeitlang traurig vor
  sich hin.)

ELSA

Mein armer Bruder!

She feigned a sorrow, asked about her
brother,
Whom she by some strange accident
had lost,
And nevermore—so said she—found
his trace.
Fruitless was all our labor for the lost
one.
When I accused the girl and uttered
threats,
Her sudden pallor, coupled with her
trembling,
Were proof of the horrid misdeed she
had done.
A horror of the maiden seized my
soul.
The right to have her hand—a right
her father gave—
I now most willingly renounced,
And took a wife who pleased my mind
and heart,
Ortrud, daughter of Radbod, Frisian
prince.
And so I raise complaint of Elsa of
Brabant:
She slew her brother: this I charge.
I now claim that this land is mine by
right,
Since I am next the noble count by
blood.
My wife, besides, is of the race that
once
Brought forth the mighty lords who
ruled our realm.
You hear this matter, sovereign! Judge
aright!

ALL THE MEN
Ha, Telramund charges heavy guilt.
His tale fills me with shuddering
dread!

THE KING
A frightful accusation you have
brought!
Is guilt so wicked even possible?

FREDERICK
O King, dream-fuddled is that foolish
maid,
Who proudly drew away her hand
from mine.
I now accucse her too of secret love.
She dreamed, perhaps, if she removed
her brother,
Then she could rule as mistress of
Brabant
And therefore rightly cast aside her
liegeman,
To openly enjoy her secret lover.

KING HENRY
Call the accused one here! For judgment
straightway shall begin. God keep me
truly wise!

HERALD
Shall judgment here be held by law of
right and might?

THE KING
I nevermore shall bear my shield
Till right prevails through gentle
might!

ALL THE MEN
No sword shall be returned to scabbard,
Till a righteous judgment rules.

THE HERALD
Where you behold the royal shield,
There righteous judgment must prevail.
And so I call both loud and clear:
Elsa, appear upon this place!
(*Elsa enters, but remains awhile at
back; then she slowly and timidly ad-
vances to the front. The ladies of her
train remain on the outer edge of the
Judgment Circle.*)

ALL THE MEN
Behold! She comes, the hapless
maiden!
Ha! how she shines forth so pure and
bright!
He who so harshly dare accuse her
Must be most sure her guilt is real!

THE KING
Are you she, Elsa of Brabant?
(*Elsa bows her head in assent.*)
Do you allow that I should be your
judge?
(*Elsa turns her head towards the King,
gazes into his eyes, and then makes
an affirmative gesture of her com-
plete trust.*)
I ask you
Then further: do you know the heavy
charge
Which here has been alleged against
you?
(*Elsa looks at Frederick and Ortrud,
shudders, and sadly inclines her head
in assent.*)
Can you meet the charge against you?
(*Elsa indicates by gesture that she can
say nothing.*)
Is this token of your guilt?
(*She gazes sadly before her.*)

ALLE MÄNNER

Wie wunderbar! Welch' seltsames Gebaren!

KÖNIG

Sag', Elsa! Was hast du mir zu vertrau'n?

ELSA

Einsam in trüben Tagen
Hab' ich zu Gott gefleht,
Des Herzens tiefstes Klagen
Ergoss ich im Gebet.
Da drang aus meinem Stöhnen,
Ein Laut so klagevoll,
Der zu gewalt'gem Tönen
Weit in die Lüfte schwoll:
Ich hört' ihn fern hin hallen,
Bis kaum mein Ohr er traf;
Mein Aug' ist zugefallen,
Ich sank in süssen Schlaf.

ALLE MÄNNER

Wie sonderbar! Träumt sie? Ist sie
entrückt?

KÖNIG

Elsa, verteid'ge dich vor dem Gericht!

ELSA

In lichter Waffen Scheine
Ein Ritter nahte da,
So tugendlicher Reine
Ich keinen noch ersah:
Ein golden Horn zur Hüften,
Gelehnet auf sein Schwert,
So trat er aus den Lüften
Zu mir, der Recke wert.
Mit züchtigem Gebaren
Gab Tröstung er mir ein:
Des Ritters will ich wahren,
Er soll mein Streiter sein!

KÖNIG UND ALLE MÄNNER

Bewahre uns des Himmels Huld,
Dass klar wir sehen, wer hier schuld!

KÖNIG

Friedrich, du ehrenwerter Mann,
Bedenke wohl, wen klagst du an?

FRIEDRICH

Mich irret nicht ihr träumerischer
Mut; .
Ihr hört, sie schwärmt von einem
Buhlen!
Wes' ich sie zeih', des' hab' ich sich'ren
Grund.

Glaubwürdig ward ihr Frevel mir be-
zeugt;
Doch eurem Zweifel durch ein Zeugnis
wehren,
Das stünde wahrlich übel meinem
Stolz!
Hier steh' ich, hier mein Schwert! Wer
wagt von euch
Zu streiten wider meiner Ehre Preis?

DIE BRABANTER

Keiner von uns! Wir streiten nur für
dich!

FRIEDRICH

Und König, du! Gedenkst du meiner
Dienste,
Wie ich im Kampf den wilden Dänen
schlug?

KÖNIG

Wie schlimm, liess' ich von dir daran
mich mahnen!
Gern geb' ich dir der höchsten Tugend
Preis;
In keiner andren Hut, als in der
deinen,
Möcht' ich die Lande wissen. Gott
allein
Soll jetzt in dieser Sache noch entschei-
den.

ALLE MÄNNER

Zum Gottesgericht! Zum Gottesgericht!
Wohlan!

KÖNIG

(zieht sein Schwert und stösst es vor
sich in die Erde)

Dich frag' ich, Friedrich, Graf von Tel-
ramund!
Willst du durch Kampf auf Leben und
auf Tod
Im Gottesgericht vertreten deine
Klage?

FRIEDRICH

Ja!

KÖNIG

Und dich nun frag' ich, Elsa von Bra-
bant!
Willst du, dass hier auf Leben und auf
Tod
Im Gottesgericht ein Kämpe für dich
streite?

ELSA

Ja!

KÖNIG

Wen wählest du zum Streiter?

FRIEDRICH

Vernehmet jetzt den Namen ihres Buhlen!

ELSA

My poor, poor brother!

ALL THE MEN

How wonderful! How strange is her
demeanor!

THE KING

Speak, Elsa! What is it you would
impart?

ELSA

Often when sad and lonely
I unto God have prayed.
My heart's most deepfelt longings
Implored celestial aid.
Among my loud lamentings
Was one whose woe so rare
Onward and upward bore it,
Far into heaven's air.
And long I heard it echo
Until it died away.
My eyes became quite heavy,
And then sweet sleep held sway.

ALL THE MEN

How singular! Curious! Is she
entranced?

THE KING

Elsa, defend yourself against the
charge!

ELSA

I saw a knight approaching
In armor gleaming bright;
His purity was dazzling,
I never viewed its like.
A golden horn beside him,
He leaned upon his sword,
Thus, suddenly I saw him,
My radiant, future lord.
His tender, gentle manner
From sorrow set me free.
I now await his coming,
My champion he shall be!

THE KING AND ALL THE MEN

May heavenly grace pour down its
light,
That we may see who stands in guilt.

THE KING

Frederick, most honor-worthy man,
Bethink you well whom you accuse.

FREDERICK

Her dreamy mood does not mislead my
mind.
You hear, she raves about a lover!
My charge is true: I stand on solid
ground.

Witness most worthy has revealed her
crime.
Yet to defend my words by using such
a witness
Would be abhorrent to my pride!
Here stand I, here my sword! Who is
it dares
Contend against the honor of my word?

THE BRABANTIANS

None of us here! We just contend for
you!

FREDERICK

And you, my King! Remember how I
served you,
Remember how I fought the furious
Danes?

THE KING

How ill, were there a need that you
remind me!
You are esteemed as virtue's fairest
flower.
My wish would only be to see this
country
Solely in your protection. God alone
Shall consummate right now this great
decision.

THE MEN

The judgment of God! The judgment
of God! Agreed!

THE KING

(drawing his sword and striking it before him into the earth)

I ask you, Frederick, Count of
Telramund!
Will you engage in life and death
encounter
Now, and entrust your cause to
heaven's judgment?

FREDERICK

Yes!

THE KING

And now I ask you, Elsa of Brabant,
Will you submit your cause, involving
life
And death, to a hero fighting under
heaven?

ELSA

Yes!

THE KING

Whom do you choose as champion?

FREDERICK

At last we'll hear the name of her
sweetheart!

DIE BRABANTER

Merket auf!

ELSA

Des Ritters will ich wahren,
Er soll mein Streiter sein!
Hört, was dem Gottgesandten
Ich biete für Gewähr:
In meines Vaters Landen
Die Krone trage er;
Mich glücklich soll ich preisen,
Nimmt er mein Gut dahin,
Will er Gemahl mich heissen,
Geb' ich ihm, was ich bin!

DIE MÄNNER

Ein schöner Preis, stünd' er in Gottes
Hand!
Wer um ihn stritt', wohl setzt' er schwe-
res Pfand!

KÖNIG

Im Mittag hoch steht schon die Sonne:
So ist es Zeit, dass nun der Ruf ergeh'.
(Der Heerrufer tritt mit den vier Trompetern vor, die er den vier Himmels-
gegenden zugewendet an die äusser-
ste Grenze des Gerichtskreises vor-
schreiten und so den Ruf blasen
lässt.)

DER HEERRUFER

Wer hier im Gotteskampf zu streiten
kam
Für Elsa von Brabant, der trete vor!

DIE MÄNNER

Ohn' Antwort ist ihr Ruf verhallt,
Um ihre Sache steht es schlecht.

FRIEDRICH

Gewahrt, ob ich sie fälschlich schalt?
Auf meiner Seite bleibt das Recht!

ELSA

Mein lieber König, lass dich bitten,
Noch einen Ruf an meinen Ritter!
Wohl weilt er fern und hört ihn nicht.

KÖNIG (zum Heerrufer)

Noch einmal rufe zum Gericht!
(Die Trompeter wiederholen den
Anruf.)

DER HEERRUFER

Wer hier im Gotteskampf zu streiten
kam
Für Elsa von Brabant, der trete vor!

DIE MÄNNER

In düst'rem Schweigen richtet Gott!

(Elsa sinkt zu inbrünstigem Gebet auf
die Kniee. Die Frauen, in Besorgnis
um ihre Herrin, treten etwas näher in
den Vordergrund.)

ELSA

Du trugest zu ihm meine Klage,
Zu mir trat er auf dein Gebot:
O Herr, nun meinem Ritter sage,
Dass er mir helf' in meiner Not!
Lass mich ihn seh'n, wie ich ihn sah,
Wie ich ihn sah, sei er mir nah!

ELSA'S FRAUEN (auf die Knie sinkend)

Herr! Sende Hilfe ihr!
Herr Gott! Höre uns!

(Lohengrin wird in der Ferne in
einem von einem Schwan gezogenen
Nachen sichtbar.)

DIE MÄNNER

Seht! Seht! Welch' ein seltsam Wun-
der! Wie? Ein Schwan?
Ein Schwan zieht einen Nachen dort
heran!
Ein Ritter drin hoch aufgerichtet steht.
Wie glänzt sein Waffenschmuck! Das
Aug' vergeht
Vor solchem Glanz! Seht, näher kommt
er an!
An einer gold'nen Kette zieht der
Schwan!

ALLE MÄNNER UND FRAUEN

Ein Wunder! Ein Wunder! Ein Wunder ist gekommen,
ein unerhörtes, nie geseh'nes Wunder!
Gegrüsst, du gottgesandter Mann!

(Während des Folgenden kommt der
Schwan mit dem Nachen vollends
am Ufer an: Lohengrin steht darin.)

LOHENGRIN

Nun sei bedankt, mein lieber Schwan!
Zieh' durch die weite Flut zurück,
Dahin, woher mich trug dein Kahn,
Kehr' wieder nur zu uns'rem Glück:
Drum sei getreu dein Dienst getan!
Leb' wohl! Leb' wohl, mein lieber
Schwan!

(Der Schwan wendet den Nachen und
schwimmt den Fluss zurück.)

THE BRABANTIANS

Mark her words!

ELSA

I now await his coming,
My champion he shall be.
He who was sent by heaven
Will freely from my hand
Win crown and full possession
Of all my father's land.
To grant him my possessions
I joyously agree;
And if he calls me consort,
His vassal let me be.

ALL THE MEN

A splendid prize, if God will show him
    grace!
He who contends plays for a heavy
    stake!

THE KING

The midday sun hangs high in
    heaven;
Now it is time to let the call go forth!

(*The herald advances with the four
    trumpeters, whom he places towards
    the four points of the compass at the
    outer edge of the judgment-circle,
    where they blow the summons.*)

THE HERALD

He who would fight on side of godly
    right
For Elsa of Brabant, let him step forth!

ALL THE MEN

No answer to the call has come!
I fear her matter goes quite ill!

FREDERICK

Observe, if I have falsely charged:
This proves that right is on my side.

ELSA

My gracious sovereign, let me beg you
Yet one more call to reach my
    champion!
He may be far and hear it not.

THE KING (*to the herald*)

Yet one more time to call him here!

(*The trumpeters blow again.*)

THE HERALD

He who in sight of God would take the
    sword
For Elsa of Brabant, let him appear!

ALL THE MEN

In gloomy silence God does judge!

(*Elsa sinks in fervent prayer on her
    knees: her ladies, concerned for her,
    come nearer to the front.*)

ELSA

Thou borest Him my cries of sorrow.
He came to me through Thy command.
O Lord, speak to my noble hero,
To help me now in time of need.
Let him be seen as he appeared.

THE LADIES (*falling on their knees*)

Lord! Send her help from on high!
Lord God! Hear our prayer!

(*Lohengrin is seen in the distance ap-
    proaching in a skiff drawn by a
    swan.*)

THE MEN

Look! look! Look, how rare a wonder!
    What? A swan!
A swan that draws a little boat this
    way!
A knight is on board: see him standing
    there!
How bright his warlike arms! My eyes
    are dazzled
By the light! See, nearer now he comes!
The swan conveys him by a chain of
    gold!
Look, ever nearer he comes, and now
    he's gained the shore!

ALL THE MEN AND WOMEN

A wonder! a wonder! a wonder is
    approaching!
Ha, a wonder never seen and never
    heard of!
All hail! all hail, you hero sent by God!

(*Here the swan-drawn skiff reaches the
    shore. Lohengrin stands within it,
    leaning on his sword. Frederick is
    speechless, Ortrud in consternation at
    sight of the swan. All bare their
    heads.*)

LOHENGRIN

Now take my thanks, beloved swan!
Sail back the watery ways again
From whence your skiff has carried me.
Come once again when fortune smiles.
Thus hold your faith to service done.
Farewell, farewell, beloved swan!

(*The swan slowly turns the skiff and
    sails back on the stream.*)

DIE MÄNNER UND FRAUEN
Wie fasst uns selig süsses Grauen,
Welch' holde Macht hält uns gebannt!
Wie ist er schön und hehr zu schauen,
Den solch' ein Wunder trug an's
    Land!

LOHENGRIN
Heil König Heinrich! Segenvoll
Mög' Gott bei deinem Schwerte steh'n!
Ruhmreich und gross dein Name soll
Von dieser Erde nie vergeh'n!

KÖNIG
Hab' Dank!Erkenn' ich recht die
    Macht,
Die dich in dieses Land gebracht,
So nahst du uns von Gott gesandt?

LOHENGRIN
Zum Kampf für eine Magd zu steh'n,
Der schwere Klage angetan,
Bin ich gesandt:nun lasst mich seh'n,
Ob ich zu recht sie treffe an!
So sprich denn, Elsa von Brabant:
Wenn ich zum Streiter dir ernannt,
Willst du wohl ohne Bang' und Grau'n
Dich meinem Schutze anvertrau'n?

ELSA
Mein Held, mein Retter! Nimm mich
    hin!
Dir geb' ich Alles, was ich bin!

LOHENGRIN
Wenn ich im Kampfe für dich siege,
Willst du, dass ich dein Gatte sei?

ELSA
Wie ich zu deinen Füssen liege,
Geb' ich dir Leib und Seele frei.

LOHENGRIN
Elsa, soll ich dein Gatte heissen,
Soll Land und Leut' ich schirmen dir,
Soll nichts mich wieder von dir reissen,
Musst Eines du geloben mir:
Nie sollst du mich befragen,
Noch Wissens Sorge tragen,
Woher ich kam der Fahrt,
Noch wie mein Nam' und Art.

ELSA
Nie, Herr, soll mir die Frage kommen!

LOHENGRIN
Elsa! Hast du mich wohl vernommen?
Nie sollst du mich befragen,
Noch Wissens Sorge tragen,
Woher ich kam der Fahrt,
Noch wie mein Nam' und Art!

ELSA
Mein Schirm! Mein Engel! Mein
    Erlöser,
Der fest an meine Unschuld glaubt!
Wie gäb' es Zweifels Schuld, die
    grösser,
Als die an dich den Glauben raubt?
Wie du mich schirmst in meiner Not,
So halt' in Treu' ich dein Gebot!

LOHENGRIN
Elsa! Ich liebe dich!

DIE MÄNNER UND FRAUEN
Welch' holde Wunder muss ich seh'n?
Ist's Zauber, der mir angetan?
Ich fühl' das Herze mir vergeh'n,
Schau' ich den hehren, wonnevollen
    Mann!

LOHENGRIN
Nun hört! Euch, Volk und Edlen mach
    ich kund:
Frei aller Schuld ist Elsa von Brabant.
Dass falsch dein Klagen, Graf von Tel-
    ramund,
Durch Gottes Urteil werd' es dir be-
    kannt!

BRABANTISCHE EDLE
Steh' ab vom Kampf! Wenn du ihn
    wagst,
Zu siegen nimmer du vermagst!
Ist er von höchster Macht geschützt,
Sag', was dein tapf'res Schwert dir
    nützt?
Steh' ab! Wir mahnen dich in Treu'!
Dein harret Unsieg, bitt're Reu'!

FRIEDRICH
Viel lieber tot als feig!
Welch' Zaubern dich auch hergeführt,
Fremdling, der mir so kühn erscheint;
Dein stolzes Droh'n mich nimmer
    rührt,
Da ich zu lügen nie vermeint:
Den Kampf mit dir drum nehm' ich
    auf,
Und hoffe Sieg nach Rechtes Lauf!

LOHENGRIN
Nun, König, ord'ne unsern Kampf!

KÖNIG
So tretet vor, zu drei für jeden
    Kämpfer,
Und messet wohl den Ring zum Streite
    ab!
(Drei sächsische Edle treten für Lohen-
grin, drei brabantische für Friedrich
vor; sie messen mit feierlichen
Schritten den Kampfplatz aus und
stecken ihn durch ihre Speere ab.)

THE MEN AND WOMEN

We feel an awe of blessed sweetness!
What gracious power holds us
  enthralled?
How beautiful and bright to look on,
This man borne here by wondrous art!

LOHENGRIN

Hail, gracious monarch! May the Lord
Let victory sit upon your sword!
Famous and powerful, your name
Shall never perish from the earth!

THE KING

Have thanks! If I do reckon right
The power that led you to this land,
You came to us as sent by God.

LOHENGRIN

I came to combat for a maid
To whom a heavy harm was done.
Thus was I sent. Now let me see
If I can tell her from the rest!
So speak then, Elsa of Brabant!
If I am named for your defense,
Will you then, void of fear and doubt,
Freely entrust yourself to me?

ELSA

My knight! My hero! Take me hence!
All, all I give you—all I am!

LOHENGRIN

If I am victor in this combat,
Will you grant that I be your mate?

ELSA

Sure as I lie right here before you
Know both my soul and body yours.

LOHENGRIN

Elsa, if I'm to be your husband,
If I protect your land and people,
If nothing is to tear me from you,
Then one thing you must promise me:
You never once shall ask me,
Nor even care to wonder
From whence I journeyed here,
Nor what my name and race!

ELSA

Lord, never shall I ask such question!

LOHENGRIN

Elsa! Say, do you understand me?
You never once shall ask me,
Nor even care to wonder,
From whence I journeyed here,
Nor what my name and race.

ELSA

My shield! My angel! My preserver,
Whose heart believes me free from
  guilt!
How could there be a doubt more
  guilty
Than that which robs belief in you?
As you will help me in my need,
So I shall follow your command!

LOHENGRIN

Elsa, my love is deep!

MEN AND WOMEN .

What winning wonder do I see?
Has someone cast a magic spell?
I feel my heart begin to fail
When I behold this wondrous man!

LOHENGRIN

Now hark! Nobles and freemen, to my
  words:
Free of all guilt is Elsa of Brabant!
Your accusation, Count of Telramund,
Through heaven's judgment you shall
  know is false!

THE NOBLES OF BRABANT

Refrain from strife, for if you dare,
You do not stand a chance to win.
If it is God protects this man
Then what avails your valiant sword?
Refrain! We counsel you in truth!
Failure awaits you, bitter rue!

FREDERICK

Much better dead than fear!
Whatever magic led you here,
Stranger, who make so bold in show,
Your scornful threats have no effect,
Since I do not intend to lie.
Your challenge then do I accept,
And hope to win through course of
  right!

LOHENGRIN

Now, sovereign, prepare us for fight!

THE KING

Step forward, then, with three for each
  contendant,
And measure well a circle round the
  field.
(*Three Saxon nobles advance for Lohengrin, and three Brabantians for
Frederick; they cross the stage with
solemn strides and measure the
ground; when the six have formed a
complete circle they drive their spears
into the ground.*)

DER HEERRUFER

Nun höret mich, und achtet wohl:
Den Kampf hier keiner stören soll!
Dem Hage bleibet abgewandt,
Denn wer nicht wahrt des Friedens
    Recht,
Der Freie büss' es mit der Hand,
Mit seinem Haupte büss' es der
    Knecht!

ALLE MÄNNER

Der Freie büss' es mit der Hand,
Mit seinem Haupte büss' es der
    Knecht!

DER HEERRUFER

Hört auch, ihr Streiter vor Gericht!
Gewahrt in Treue Kampfes Pflicht!
Durch bösen Zaubers List und Trug
Stört nicht des Urteils Eigenschaft:
Gott richtet euch nach Recht und Fug,
So trauet ihm, nicht eurer Kraft!

LOHENGRIN UND FRIEDRICH

Gott richte mich nach Recht und Fug,
So trau' ich ihm, nicht meiner Kraft!

DER KÖNIG

Mein Herr und Gott, nun ruf' ich dich,
Dass du dem Kampf zugegen sei'st!
Durch Schwertes Sieg ein Urteil sprich,
Das Trug und Wahrheit klar erweist.
Des Reinen Arm gib Heldenkraft,
Des Falschen Stärke sei erschlafft:
So hilf uns, Gott, zu dieser Frist,
Weil un'sre Weisheit Einfalt ist!

ELSA UND LOHENGRIN

Du kündest nun dein wahr' Gericht,
Mein Gott und Herr, drum zag' ich
    nicht!

FRIEDRICH

Ich geh' in Treu' vor dein Gericht!
Herr Gott, nun verlass mein' Ehre
    nicht!

ORTRUD

Ich baue fest auf sein Kraft,
Die, wo er kämpft, ihm Sieg verschafft.

ALLE MÄNNER

Des Reinen Arm gib Heldenkraft,
Des Falschen Stärke sei erschlafft;
So künde nun dein wahr Gericht,
Du Herr und Gott, nun zög're nicht!

ALLE FRAUEN

Herr, mein Gott, segne ihn!
(Auf das Zeichen des Heerrufers fallen
    die Heerhörner mit einem langen
    Kampfrufe ein. Der König zieht sein
Schwert aus der Erde und schlägt
    damit dreimal auf den an der Eiche
    aufgehängten Schild. Kampf Lohen-
    grins und Friedrichs. Lohengrin
    streckt Friedrich nieder.)

LOHENGRIN
(das Schwert auf Friedrichs Hals set-
    zend)

Durch Gottes Sieg ist jetzt dein Leben
    mein:
Ich schenk' es dir, mög'st du der Reu'
    es weih'n!
(Alle Männer nehmen ihre Schwerter
    wieder an sich und stossen sie in die
    Scheiden: die Kampfzeugen ziehen
    die Speere aus der Erde: der König
    nimmt seinen Schild von der Eiche.
    Alles stürzt jubelnd nach der Mitte
    und erfüllt so den vorherigen Kampf-
    kreis. Elsa eilt auf Lohengrin zu.)

KÖNIG, MÄNNER UND FRAUEN

Sieg! Sieg! Heil dir, Held!

ELSA

O fänd' ich Jubelweisen,
Deinem Ruhme gleich,
Dich würdig zu preisen,
An höchstem Lobe reich!
In dir muss ich vergehen,
Vor dir schwind' ich dahin!
Soll ich mich selig sehen,
Nimm Alles was ich bin!

LOHENGRIN

Den Sieg hab' ich erstritten
Durch deine Rein' allein;
Nun soll, was du gelitten,
Dir reich vergolten sein!

FRIEDRICH

Weh' mich hat Gott geschlagen,
Durch ihn ich sieglos bin!
Am Heil muss ich verzagen,
Mein' Ruhm und Ehr' ist hin!

ORTRUD

Weh' mich hat Gott geschlagen,
Durch den ich machtlos bin?
Sollt' ich vor ihm verzagen,
Wär' all' mein Hoffen hin?

DER KÖNIG, MÄNNER UND FRAUEN

Ertöne, Siegesweise,
Dem Helden laut zum höchsten Preise!
Ruhm deiner Fahrt!
Preis deinem Kommen!
Heil deiner Art,
Schützer der Frommen!

THE HERALD

Now hear my words and mark me well!
Let none intrude upon this fight!
The space enclosed is out of bounds;
If any man disturbs the peace,
If freeman he shall lose his hand,
But if a churl he pays with his head!

ALL THE MEN

If freeman he shall lose his hand,
But if a churl he pays with his head!

THE HERALD

Hear too, contenders for the right!
Be fair and hold to combat rules!
Deceitful fraud of magic art
Must not disturb fair judgment's laws!
So trust His strength, and not your
      own!
God judges you in right and law.

LOHENGRIN AND FREDERICK

God judge me after right and law!
I trust His strength, and not my own!

THE KING

My Lord and God, I call on Thee,
Asking Thy presence at our strife!
Speak forth Thy sentence through the
      sword,
Let truth and falsehood clearly show.
Give him who's pure heroic strength
From falsehood take away the might.
So help us God, this time of times,
For all our wisdom is but folly!

ELSA AND LOHENGRIN

Make known to me Thy true decree,
And then, my God, I have no fear!

FREDERICK

Within Thy light shall I see light!
Lord God, let not my honor find a
      stain!

ORTRUD

I build my hope upon his strength,
Who when he fights, can never fail.

ALL THE MEN

Give him who's pure heroic strength,
From falsehood take away the might.
Make known to us Thy true decree,
O Lord and God, delay it not.

ALL THE WOMEN

My Lord and God, bless the knight!
(On a sign from the herald, the trum-
peters blow the call to battle. The
King draws his sword out of the

ground and strikes it three times on
his shield that hangs on the oak. The
combatants step into the circle and
begin. Lohengrin fells Frederick to
the earth.)

LOHENGRIN

(the point of his sword at Frederick's
throat)

Through might of God your life
belongs to me.
I spare that life: keep it to cleanse your
sin!

(All the men resume their swords, and
thrust them back into their scab-
bards. The seconds draw out the
spears, and the King takes down his
shield from the oak. All triumphantly
rush to the center where the fight
took place. Elsa hastens to Lohengrin.)

THE MEN AND WOMEN

Hail! hail! hail! great hero!

ELSA

Oh, could I make my praises
Equal to your fame,
Most worthy of heroes,
Most rich in highest praise!
Near you am I as nothing,
Near you am I the least.
So that I may be blessed,
Take all things, all I am.

LOHENGRIN

The power that made me conquer
Came through your purity!
But now for what you suffered
Your recompense is rich.

FREDERICK

Woe! God has caused my downfall,
Through Him my might is gone!
All cure I must despair of!
My name and fame are done!

ORTRUD

Who is't that caused his downfall,
And made me mightless too?
His cure should I despair of,
And banish all my hopes?

THE KING, MEN AND WOMEN

Sing loudly, songs of victory,
To him most worthy of our praises!
Fame to your deed!
Praise to your coming!
Hail to your race!
Shield of the stainless!

Dich nur besingen wir,
Dir schallen uns're Lieder!
Nie kehrt ein Held gleich dir
Zu diesen Landen wieder.

(*Friedrich sinkt zu Ortrud's Füssen
ohnmächtig zusammen. Junge
Männer erheben Lohengrin auf
seinen Schild und Elsa auf den Schild
des Königs, auf welchen zuvor meh-
rere ihre Mäntel gebreitet haben: so
werden beide unter Jauchzen da-
vongetragen.*)

ZWEITER AUFZUG

*In der Burg von Antwerpen. In der
Mitte des Hintergrundes der Palas
(Ritterwohnung), die Kemenate
(Frauenwohnung) im Vordergrunde
links; rechts im Vordergrunde die
Pforte des Münsters; ebenda im Hin-
tergrunde das Turmtor.*

FRIEDRICH (*sich rasch erhebend*)

Erhebe dich, Genossin meiner
    Schmach!
Der junge Tag darf hier uns nicht
    mehr sehn.

ORTRUD

Ich kann nicht fort, hieher bin ich ge-
    bannt,
Aus diesem Glanz des Festes unsrer
    Feinde
Lass saugen mich ein furchtbar tödlich
    Gift,
Das uns're Schmach und ihre Freuden
    ende!

FRIEDRICH

Du fürchterliches Weib, was bannt
    mich noch
In deine Nähe? Warum lass ich dich
    nicht
Allein, und fliehe fort, dahin, dahin,
Wo mein Gewissen Ruhe wieder
    fänd'?
Durch dich musst' ich verlieren
Mein' Ehr', all meinen Ruhm:
Nie soll mich Lob mehr zieren,
Schmach ist mein Heldentum!
Die Acht ist mir gesprochen,
Zertrümmert liegt mein Schwert,
Mein Wappen ward zerbrochen,
Verflucht mein Vaterherd!
Wohin ich nun mich wende,
Geflohn, gefehmt, bin ich,
Dass ihn mein Blick nicht schände,

Flieht selbst der Räuber mich.
O hätt' ich Tod erkoren,
Da ich so elend bin!
Mein' Ehr' hab' ich verloren,
Mein' Ehr', mein' Ehr' ist hin!

(*Er stürzt zu Boden.*)

ORTRUD

Was macht dich in so wilder Klage
    doch vergeh'n?

FRIEDRICH

Dass mir die Waffe selbst geraubt,
Mit der ich dich erschlüg'!

ORTRUD

Friedreicher Graf von Telramund!
Weshalb misstraust du mir?

FRIEDRICH

Du fragst? War's nicht dein Zeugnis,
    deine Kunde,
Die mich bestrickt, die Reine zu ver-
    klagen?
Die du im düst'ren Wald zu Haus, logst
    du
Mir nicht, von deinem wilden Schlosse
    aus
Die Untat habest du verüben seh'n?
Mit eig'nem Aug', wie Elsa selbst den
    Bruder
Im Weiher dort ertränkt? Umstrick-
    test du
Mein stolzes Herz durch die Weis-
    sagung nicht,
Bald würde Radbod's alter Fürsten-
    stamm
Von neuem grünen und herrschen in
    Brabant?
Bewogst du so mich nicht von Elsa's
    Hand,
Der Reinen, abzusteh'n, und dich zum
    Weib
Zu nehmen, weil du Radbod's letzter
    Spross?

ORTRUD

Ha, wie tödlich du mich kränkst!
Dies Alles, ja! ich sagt' und zeugt' es
    dir!

You only do we sing
In sounding songs and praises!
Our land will never know again
So great a hero!

(*Frederick falls senseless at the feet of Ortrud. Youths raise Lohengrin upon his shield, and Elsa upon the shield of the King, upon which several have spread their mantles; both are borne away amid general rejoicing.*)

ACT TWO

The citadel of Antwerp; at the back the "Palas" (where the knights dwell); in the foreground the Kemenate (dwelling of women); the Minster, right. It is night, and Ortrud and Frederick, both poorly garbed, are seated on the Minster steps. Frederick is musing gloomily, Ortrud gazing fixedly at the windows of the Palas, which is brightly illuminated.

FREDERICK (*rising suddenly*)

Arouse yourself, companion of my shame!
The dawning day dare see us here no more.

ORTRUD

I cannot leave, for here I am enchained,
I love to watch my foes while they are feasting
And therefrom suck a fearful deadly bane
That ends our shame and all their joy together!

FREDERICK

O woman dire and fell! what is it binds me
To your presence? Oh, why did I not shun your sight,
And fly away, away, from hence,
To where once more my conscience is at rest!
Through you I've lost my honor,
My honor and my fame.
No more shall praise adorn me;
Shame is my herohood,
And scorn henceforth my dower.
In pieces lies my sword,
My scutcheon has been spotted,
My father's house is cursed!
No matter where I wander,
Abhorred and shunned am I;
For fear my glance might sully,

Even the robbers flee.
Through you, through you, gone is my honor,
My honor and my fame.
No more shall praises adorn me,
Shame is my herohood!
And scorn henceforth my dower.
In pieces lies my sword,
My scutcheon has been spotted,
My father's house is cursed!
Great is my wretched sorrow,
I should have chosen death!
My name, my honor is departed,
My name and fame are gone!

(*He throws himself on the ground.*)

ORTRUD

Why do you eat your heart by making wild complaints?

FREDERICK

Curst one, because I even lack
A sword to strike you dead!

ORTRUD

Frederick, Count of Telramund! why this mistrust in me?

FREDERICK

You ask? Was it not your witness, your report,
Which made me accuse one innocent of evil?
When in your gloomy woodland home, did you
Not lie, by telling me that from your tower
You spied how Elsa did that deed of ill?
Your very eyes, you said, observed the girl
Drown her brother in the tarn. Did not
Your prophecies entangle my heart in my pride;
Soon would the ancient, princely Radbod branch
Put forth anew, and would lord it in Brabant?
And did you not beguile me from the hand
Of Elsa, who is pure, to take you
For my consort, as the last of Radbod's race?

ORTRUD

Ha, you make me deathly sick!
Most truly, yes, all this I said and proved.

FRIEDRICH

Und machtest mich, dess' Name hoch-
    geehrt,
Dess' Leben aller höchsten Tugend
    Preis,
Zu deiner Lüge schändlichem Ge-
    nossen?

ORTRUD

Wer log?

FRIEDRICH

Du! Hat nicht durch sein Gericht
Gott mich dafür geschlagen?

ORTRUD

Gott?

FRIEDRICH

Entsetzlich! Wie tönt aus deinem
    Mund furchtbar der Name!

ORTRUD

Ha, nennst du deine Feigheit Gott?

FRIEDRICH

Ortrud!

ORTRUD

Willst du mir droh'n? Mir, einem
    Weibe, droh'n?
O Feiger! hättest du so grimmig ihm
    gedroht,
Der jetzt dich in das Elend schickt.
Wohl hättest Sieg für Schande du er-
    kauft!
Ha, wer ihm zu entgegnen wüsst', der
    fänd'
Ihn schwächer als ein Kind!

FRIEDRICH

Je schwächer er, desto gewalt'ger
    kämpfte Gottes Kraft.

ORTRUD

Gottes Kraft? Ha! Ha!
Gib hier mir Macht, und sicher zeig'
    ich dir.
Welch' schwacher Gott es ist, der ihn
    beschützt.

FRIEDRICH

Du wilde Seherin, wie willst du doch
Geheimnisvoll den Geist mir neu be-
    rücken!

ORTRUD

(auf den Palas deutend, in dem das
    Licht verlöscht ist)
Die Schwelger streckten sich zur
    üpp'gen Ruh'.
Setz' dich zur Seite mir! Die Stund' ist
    da,

Wo dir mein Seherauge leuchten soll.
Weisst du, wer dieser Held, den hier
Ein Schwan gezogen an das Land?

FRIEDRICH

Nein!

ORTRUD

Was gäbst du doch, es zu erfahren,
Wenn ich dir sag', ist er gezwungen
Zu nennen wie sein Nam' und Art,
All seine Macht zu Ende ist,
Die mühvoll ihm ein Zauber leiht.

FRIEDRICH

Ha! Dann begriff' ich sein Verbot.

ORTRUD

Nun hör! Niemand hier hat Gewalt
Ihm das Geheimniss zu entreissen,
Als die, der er so streng verbot
Die Frage je an ihn zu tun.

FRIEDRICH

So gält' es, Elsa zu verleiten,
Dass sie die Frag' ihm nicht erliess'?

ORTRUD

Ha, wie begreifst du schnell und wohl!

FRIEDRICH

Doch wie soll das gelingen?

ORTRUD

Hör'!
Vor allem gilt's von hinnen nicht
Zu flieh'n: drum schärfe deinen Witz!
Gerechten Argwohn ihr zu wecken,
Tritt vor, klag' ihn des Zaubers an,
Mit dem er das Gericht getäuscht!

FRIEDRICH

Ha! Trug und Zaubers List!

ORTRUD

Missglückt's, so bleibt ein Mittel der
    Gewalt.

FRIEDRICH

Gewalt?

ORTRUD

Umsonst nicht bin ich in
Geheimsten Künsten tief erfahren;
Drum achte wohl, was ich dir sage!
Jed' Wesen, das durch Zauber stark,
Wird ihm des Leibes kleinstes Glied
Entrissen nur, muss sich alsbald
Ohmächtig zeigen, wie es ist.

FRIEDRICH

Ha, sprächst du wahr!

FREDERICK

You made of me, whose name was
  nobly known,
Whose life was counted fairest virtue's
  flower,
The vile accomplice of your shameless
  lying.

ORTRUD

Who lied?

FREDERICK

You! That is the reason why,
God and His judgment struck me!

ORTRUD

God?

FREDERICK

How horrid!
To hear you name the name of God
  sounds most frightful!

ORTRUD

Ha, do you call your cowardice God?

FREDERICK

Ortrud!

ORTRUD

You threaten me, who am a woman!
O, you coward! Had you been so
  fierce in threats
To him who brought you to your
  wretched fate,
Victory, instead of shame, would now
  be yours!
Ha, he who only knew the way
Would find him weaker than a child!

FREDERICK

The weaker he,
The more his power must have come
  from God.

ORTRUD

Come from God! Ha, ha!
Give me the power and I will show
  you proof
How weak a God it is that fights for
  him.

FREDERICK

You savage seeress, you think that by
Your wily ways you may once more
  entice me?

ORTRUD

(pointing to the Palas, where the lights
  are now extinguished)

The revelers lie outstretched in sottish
  rest;
Come, sit here by my side! The hour
  has come

For my prophetic eyes to lend you
  light!
Do you know who he is, that hero
Brought here by a magic swan?

FREDERICK

No!

ORTRUD

What would you give to know about
  him?
What if I said, if one compels him
To utter forth his name and birth,
Then, all that might is at an end
Which he had won by magic art.

FREDERICK

Ha, his forbidding then made sense.

ORTRUD

Now hear! No one here has the power
To wrest the secret from his bosom
But she, to whom he gave command
To never seek to question him.

FREDERICK

Our need then must be to persuade her
To put the question to the knight.

ORTRUD

How fast and well you apprehend!

FREDERICK

Yet how is that accomplished?

ORTRUD

Hear!
Above all else we must not try
To flee; so sharpen well your wits!
Arouse in her a just suspicion.
Step forth, charge him with magic art,
Whereby he has perverted truth.

FREDERICK

Ha! Fraud and magic art!

ORTRUD

At worst,
There still remains the means of force.

FREDERICK

Of force!

ORTRUD

It's not for nothing I am skilled
In deepest secret magic;
So heed the words that I shall tell you:
One given strength by magic art
Will, if the slightest piece of flesh
  is torn from him, be seen
Completely shorn of power, as he is.

FREDERICK

Ha, were that true!

ORTRUD

O hättest du
Im Kampf nur einen Finger ihm,
Ja, eines Fingers Glied entschlagen,
Der Held, er war in deiner Macht!

FRIEDRICH

Entsetzlich! Ha, was lässest du mich
hören!
Durch Gott geschlagen wähnt' ich
mich:
Nun liess durch Trug sich das Gericht
betören,
Durch Zaubers List verlor mein' Ehre
ich!
Doch meine Schande könnt' ich rächen,
Bezeugen könnt' ich meine Treu'?
Des Buhlen Trug, ich könnt' ihn
brechen,
Und meine Ehr' gewönn' ich neu!
O Weib, das in der Nacht ich vor mir
seh',
Betrügst du jetzt mich noch, dann weh
dir! Weh!

ORTRUD

Ha, wie du rasest! Ruhig und be-
sonnen!
So lehr' ich dich der Rache süsse
Wonnen!

ORTRUD UND FRIEDRICH

Der Rache Werk sei nun beschworen
Aus meines Busens wilder Nacht!
Die ihr in süssem Schlaf verloren,
Wisst, dass für euch das Unheil wacht!

(*Elsa ist auf dem Söller der Kemenate
erschienen.*)

ELSA

Euch Lüften, die mein Klagen
So traurig oft erfüllt,
Euch muss ich dankend sagen,
Wie sich mein Glück enthüllt.

ORTRUD

Sie ist es!

FRIEDRICH

Elsa!

ELSA

Durch euch kam er gezogen,
Ihr lächeltet der Fahrt;
Auf wilden Meereswogen
Habt ihr ihn treu bewahrt.

ORTRUD

Der Stunde soll sie fluchen,
In der sie jetzt mein Blick gewahrt!

ELSA

Zu trocknen meine Zähren
Hab' ich euch oft gemüht:
Wollt Kühlung nun gewähren
Der Wang' in Lieb' erglüht!

ORTRUD

Hinweg!
Entfern' ein Kleines dich von hier!

FRIEDRICH

Warum?

ORTRUD

Sie ist für mich—ihr Held gehöre dir!
(*Friedrich entfernt sich in den Hinter-
grund.*)
Elsa!

ELSA

Wer ruft? Wie schauerlich und klagend
Ertönt mein Name durch die Nacht?

ORTRUD

Elsa!
Ist meine Stimme dir so fremd?
Willst du die Ärmste ganz verleugnen,
Die du in's fernste Elend schickst?

ELSA

Ortrud? bist du's? Was machst du hier,
Unglücklich Weib?

ORTRUD

"Unglücklich Weib!"
Wohl hast du recht mich so zu
nennen!
In ferner Einsamkeit des Waldes,
Wo still und friedsam ich gelebt,
Was tat ich dir? was tat ich dir?
Freudlos, das Unglück nur beweinend,
Das lang belastet meinen Stamm,
Was tat ich dir? was tat ich dir?

ELSA

Um Gott, was klagest du mich an?
War ich es, die dir Leid gebracht?

ORTRUD

Wie könntest du fürwahr mir neiden
Das Glück, dass mich zum Weib
erwählt
Der Mann, den du so gern verschmäht?

ELSA

Allgüt'ger Gott! Was soll mir das?

ORTRUD

Musst' ihn unsel'ger Wahn betören,
Dich Reine einer Schuld zu zeih'n
Von Reu' ist nun sein Herz zerrissen,
Zu grimmer Buss' ist er verdammt.

ORTRUD

Oh had you
While you fought, but torn a finger off,
Yes, or the smallest bit of finger,
The knight would then be in your
    power!

FREDERICK

How frightful! What's this you let me
    hark to?
I thought I had been struck by God,
Yet now I know that justice fell by
    falsehood,
Through magic art my honor came to
    grief.
Yet can I clear my name by vengeance,
And throw a light upon my worth?
I'd break the fraud of those two lovers,
And win my honor back again!
O wife I see before me in the dark,
If you betray me still, then, woe's you,
    woe!

ORTRUD

Ha, you are raving! Keep calm and
    collected!
And I will teach you sweetest joys of
    vengeance!

ORTRUD AND FREDERICK

Let work of vengeance now be sworn to
From out my bosom's bitter night!
You who are lost in sweetest slumber,
Know that for you wait bane and
    blight!

(*Elsa, in a white dress, appears on the
    balcony of the Kemenate, which she
    leans over.*)

ELSA

You breezes, filled so often
With sounds of my lament,
Let me with thanks now tell you
What fortune you have sent.

ORTRUD

It is she!

FREDERICK

Elsa!

ELSA

You kindly drew him seaward,
You smiled upon his path;
You guided him in safety,
Despite the wild waves' wrath.

ORTRUD

She'll find that hour accursed
In which she chanced to see my face.

ELSA

And just as when I've called you
You dried my tears of woe,
So now bestow your cooling
On cheek with love aglow!

ORTRUD

Away!
Keep off a little way from here!

FREDERICK

But why?

ORTRUD

She is for me: her hero is for you!
        (*Frederick disappears.*)
Elsa!

ELSA

Who calls? How mournfully
    complaining
I hear my name resound at night!

ORTRUD

Elsa!
Why should my name sound strange to
    you?
Will you disclaim that wretched soul
Who was brought by you to utmost
    woe?

ELSA

Ortrud! it's you? Why are you here,
Woman of woe?

ORTRUD

"Woman of woe?"
You have good reason so to name me!
Within the fastness of the forest,
Where peace and quiet were my lot,
I harmed you not, I harmed you not.
Joyless, bewailing only sorrows
That long had fallen on my house,
What did I do? I harmed you not.

ELSA

Good heaven! why make complaint
    to me?
Was I the one who brought your woe?

ORTRUD

What reason did you have to envy
That luck that made me chosen wife
To one whom you so gladly spurned?

ELSA

All gracious God! What's this to me?

ORTRUD

If he, misled by wretched fancy,
Thought you, the guiltless, full of guilt,
His heart is torn by sore repentance,
The punishment he takes is fierce.

ELSA

Gerechter Gott!

ORTRUD

O du bist glücklich!
Nach kurzem, unschuldsüssem Leiden,
Siehst lächeln du das Leben nur;
Von mir darfst selig du dich scheiden,
Mich schickst du auf des Todes Spur,
Dass meines Jammers trüber Schein
Nie kehr' in deine Feste ein.

ELSA

Wie schlecht ich deine Güte priese,
Allmächt'ger, der mich so beglückt,
Wenn ich das Unglück von mir stiesse,
Das sich im Staube vor mir bückt!
O nimmer! Ortrud! Harre mein!
Ich selber lass' dich zu mir ein.
(*Sie geht eilig in die Kemenate
zurück.*)

ORTRUD

Entweihte Götter! Helft jetzt meiner
Rache!
Bestraft die Schmach, die hier euch an-
getan!
Stärkt mich im Dienst eurer heil'gen
Sache!
Vernichtet der Abtrünn'gen schnöden
Wahn!
Wodan! Dich Starken rufe ich!
Freia! Erhab'ne, höre mich!
Segnet mir Trug und Heuchelei,
Dass glücklich meine Rache sei!

ELSA (*noch ausserhalb*)

Ortrud, wo bist du?
(*Elsa und zwei Mägde mit Lichten
treten aus der unteren Tür auf.*)

ORTRUD

Hier, zu deinen Füssen.

ELSA

Hilf Gott! So muss ich dich erblicken,
Die ich in Stolz und Pracht nur sah!
Es will das Herze mir ersticken,
Seh' ich so niedrig dich mir nah!
Steh' auf! O, spare mir dein Bitten!
Trugst du mir Hass, verzeih ich dir;
Was du schon jetzt durch mich gelitten,
Das, bitte ich, verzeih' auch mir!

ORTRUD

O habe dank für so viel Güte!

ELSA

Der morgen nun mein Gatte heisst,
Anfleh' ich sein liebreich Gemüte,
Dass Friedrich auch er Gnad' erweist.

ORTRUD

Du fesselst mich in Dankes Banden.

ELSA

In Früh'n lass mich bereit dich seh'n!
Geschmückt mit prächtigen Gewan-
den,
Sollst du mit mir zum Münster geh'n.
Dort harre ich des Helden mein,
Vor Gott sein Eh'gemahl zu sein.

ORTRUD

Wie kann ich solche Huld dir lohnen,
Da machtlos ich und elend bin?
Soll ich in Gnaden bei dir wohnen,
Stets bleibe ich die Bettlerin!
Nur eine Kraft ist mir geblieben,
Sie raubte mir kein Machtgebot;
Durch sie vielleicht schütz' ich dein
Leben,
Bewahr' es vor der Reue Not.

ELSA

Wie meinst du?

ORTRUD

Wohl dass ich dich warne,
Zu blind nicht deinem Glück zu trau'n;
Dass nicht ein Unheil dich umgarne,
Lass mich für dich zur Zukunft
schau'n.

ELSA

Welch' Unheil?

ORTRUD

Könntest du erfassen,
Wie dessen Art so wundersam,
Der nie dich möge so verlassen,
Wie er durch Zauber zu dir kam.

ELSA

Du Ärmste kannst wohl nie ermessen,
Wie zweifellos mein Herze liebt?
Du hast wohl nie das Glück besessen,
Das sich uns nur durch Glauben gibt?
Kehr' bei mir ein! Lass mich dich leh-
ren,
Wie süss die Wonne reinster Treu'!
Lass zu dem Glauben dich bekehren:
Es gibt ein Glück, das ohne Reu'!

ORTRUD (*für sich*)

Ha! dieser Stolz, er soll mich lehren,
Wie ich bekämpfe ihre Treu',
Gen ihn will ich die Waffen kehren,

ELSA

Have mercy, heaven!

ORTRUD

Oh, you are happy!
Your guiltless suffering went by
  quickly.
Your life beholds a cloudless sky.
You now may blithely leave my
  presence
And send me on my way to death,
So that the shadow of my woe
May never interrupt your feasts!

ELSA

How ill would I have prized Thy
  goodness,
Almighty One who blessed me so,
If I repelled this wretched woman
Who bows before me in the dust!
Oh never! Ortrud! Wait for me!
Myself will come and let you in!
(She hastens back into the Kemenate.)

ORTRUD

You gods most holy help me to my
  vengeance!
Requite the shame which you have
  suffered here!
Make me more strong in your sacred
  service!
Demolish the dreams of the renegade!
Wodan! On thee, Great Power, I call!
Freia! Renowned one, hear my cry!
Bless my deceit and treachery.
Untrammeled let my vengeance work!

ELSA (still outside)

Ortrud? Where are you?
(Elsa, with two maids bearing lights,
  enters.)

ORTRUD

Here, prostrate before you!

ELSA

Oh God! That I should thus behold
  you
Whom once I saw in splendid pride!
My heart will choke me in my bosom
Just seeing you abased like this!
Get up! O, spare me all this pleading!
Did you bear me hate, I pardon you;
Whatever too I've made you suffer,
That, if you will, forgive me too.

ORTRUD

Oh have my thanks for so much
  goodness!

ELSA

Tomorrow, on my bridal day,
I'll plead with his liberal nature
That Frederick too may have this
  grace.

ORTRUD

You fetter me with bonds of goodness!

ELSA

By early morning be prepared,
Adorned in beautiful attirement
We'll walk together to the church.
There I'll await my hero groom,
To be his bride in sight of God!

ORTRUD

How can I recompense such goodness
Since I am poor and powerless?
Though through your grace I stay right
  by you,
I still remain the beggarmaid!
There is a power I'm still possessed of,
No word of might bereft it me.
This way, perhaps, I may protect
And save you from a sore regret.

ELSA

What say you?

ORTRUD

Just attend my warning,
Do not too blindly trust your luck,
Just so a mishap may not hurt you.
Now let me scry your future fate.

ELSA

What mishap?

ORTRUD

Have you never wondered
How with an art so marvelous,
This man might leave you through that
  magic,
Through that same art whereby he
  came?

ELSA

Poor woman, you can never measure
How free from doubt my loving heart,
Nor have you known the happiness
That can only come to us through
  faith.
Come in with me! Let me but teach
  you
How sweet the joy of purest trust!
Let faith convert you to this knowledge.
There truly is a happiness without
  regret!

ORTRUD (aside)

Ha! What a pride! I'll let it teach me
How to combat this faith of hers.
Against it I will turn the weapons:

Durch ihren Hochmut werd' ihr Reu'!
(*Elsa führt Ortrud in die Kemenate,
die Mägde leuchten voran. Friedrich
tritt aus dem Hintergrunde hervor.*)..

FRIEDRICH

So zieht das Unheil in dies Haus!
Vollführe, Weib, was deine List er-
sonnen,
Dein Werk zu hemmen fühl' ich keine
Macht.
Das Unheil hat mit meinem Fall be
gonnen,
Nun stürzet nach, die mich dahin gebracht!
Nur Eines seh' ich mahnend vor mir
steh'n:
Der Räuber meiner Ehre soll vergeh'n!
*Der Tag bricht vollends an. Türmer
blasen ein Morgenlied, von einem
entfernteren Turme wird geantwor-
tet. Dann schreiten die vier Heerhornbläser aus dem Palas und blasen
den Königsruf, worauf sie wieder
zurückgehen. Friedrich hat sich
hinter einem Mauervorsprung am
Münster verborgen. Aus dem Burg-
hofe und durch das Turmtor
kommen nun brabantische Edle und
Mannen vor dem Münster zusammen.*

DIE EDLEN UND MANNEN

In Früh'n versammelt uns der Ruf,
Gar viel verheisset wohl der Tag!
Der hier so hehre Wunder schuf,
Manch' neue Tat vollbringen mag.

(*Der Heerrufer schreitet mit den vier
Heerhornbläsern aus dem Palas her-
aus. Sie blasen den Ruf von Neuem.*)

DER HEERRUFER

Des Königs Wort und Will' tu'ich euch
kund;
Drum achtet wohl, was euch durch
mich er sagt!
In Bann und Acht ist Friedrich Telramund,
Weil untreu er den Gotteskampf
gewagt:
Wer sein noch pflegt, wer sich zu ihm
gesellt,
Nach Reiches Recht derselben Acht
verfällt.

DIE MÄNNER

Fluch ihm, dem Ungetreuen,
Den Gottes Urteil traf!
Ihn soll der Reine scheuen,
Es flieh' ihn Ruh' und Schlaf!

DER HEERRUFER

Und weiter kündet euch der König an,
Dass er den fremden, gottgesandten
Mann,
Den Elsa zum Gemahle sich ersehnt,
Mit Land und Krone von Brabant be-
lehnt.
Doch will der Held nicht Herzog sein
genannt,
Ihr sollt ihn heissen: Schützer von Bra-
bant!

DIE MÄNNER

Hoch der ersehnte Mann,
Heil ihm, den Gott gesandt!
Treu sind wir untertan
Dem Schützer von Brabant!

DER HEERRUFER

Nun hört, was er durch mich euch
sagen lässt!
Heut' feiert er mit euch sein Hoch-
zeitsfest,
Doch morgen sollt ihr kampfgerüstet
nah'n,
Zur Heeresfolg' dem König untertan.
Er selbst verschmäht der süssen Ruh'
zu pflegen,
Er führt euch an zu hehren Ruhmes
Segen!
(*Der Heerrufer geht mit den vier
Trompetern in den Palas zurück.*)

DIE MÄNNER

Zum Streite säumet nicht,
Führt euch der Hehre an!
Wer mutig mit ihm ficht,
Dem lacht des Ruhmes Bahn.
Von Gott ist er gesandt
Zur Grösse von Brabant!

(*Im Vordergrunde treten vier Edle
zusammen.*)

DER DRITTE EDLE

Nun hört, dem Lande will er uns ent-
führen!

DER ZWEITE

Gen einen Feind, der uns noch nie be-
droht?

DER VIERTE

Solch kühn Beginnen sollt' ihm nicht
gebühren.

DER ERSTE

Wer wehret ihm, wenn er die Fahrt ge-
bot?
FRIEDRICH (*enthüllt sein Haupt*)
Ich!

Her pride shall bring about her fall!

(*Elsa leads Ortrud into the Kemenate,
lighted by the servants. Day has be-
gun to dawn. Frederick comes forward.*)

FREDERICK

So enters mischief in that house!
O woman, act what you have subtly
plotted.
I have no might to hinder what you do.
My downfall was the start of all this
mischief.
Down let them plunge who brought me
to my fall!
There's only one thing before my eyes:
The robbers of my honor shall be
doomed!

*Daylight. A warder gives the morning
signal, which is answered from a distant tower. The four trumpeters then
come out of the Palas, and, after
sounding the royal summons, retire.
Frederick has concealed himself be-
hind a buttress of the Minster. From
the gates of the fortress and the town
nobles of Brabant and retainers advance and greet each other.*

NOBLES AND RETAINERS

The early summons brings us here.
Great deeds are promised on this day.
The knight who wrought such wonders
here
May soon bring forth a new array.

(*Herald, with his four trumpeters, advances from the Palas to the eleva-
tion in front of it. Again the royal
summons is sounded.*)

HERALD

Our sovereign's word and will now are
proclaimed.
Heed well the words he speaks to you
through me.
Outlawed and banned is Frederick
Telramund,
Because he knew his guilt yet dared to
fight.
Who shelters him, who treats him as
a friend
Will be by selfsame royal rule con-
demned.

THE MEN

Curse him! the man of falsehood,
Who bears the ban of God!
Let all the righteous shun him!
Dispel his rest and sleep!

HERALD

And further news the king makes
known to you,
That to the stranger sent to us by God,
The man who sought for Elsa's maiden
hand,
Our king has granted both a crown and
land.
The hero, though, shall not be named a
duke,
But all shall call him Guardian of
Brabant!

THE MEN

Hail, hail to the longed for man!
Hail him, whom God has sent!
True is our service
To the Guardian of Brabant!

HERALD

Now hear what he through me would
have you know!
This day he holds with you his wed-
ding feast,
But on the morrow be in battle trim
To follow him as soldiers of the king,
While he himself disdains the balm of
sweet rest
To lead you forth to topmost height of
glory!

(*With trumpeters, Herald returns into
Palas.*)

THE MEN

Be ready for the fight.
The hero leads you forth!
Who boldly stands with him
Will win renown and worth!
From God has he been sent
To glorify Brabant!

(*Four nobles advance.*)

THIRD NOBLE

Hear that! He plans to lead us from
our country!

SECOND NOBLE

Against a foe who never threatened us?

FOURTH NOBLE

Such bold beginning looks too ill
beseeming.

FIRST NOBLE

Who'll stand to him when he is in
command?

FREDERICK (*uncovers his head*)

I!

DIE VIER EDLEN

Ha! Wer bist du? Friedrich! Seh' ich
recht?
Du wagst dich her, zur Beute jedem
Knecht?

FRIEDRICH

Gar bald will ich wohl weiter noch
mich wagen,
Vor euern Augen soll es leuchtend
tagen!
Der euch so kühn die Heerfahrt ange-
sagt,
Der sei von mir des Gottestrugs
beklagt!

DIE VIER EDLEN

Was hör' ich! Rasender! Was hast du
vor?
Verlor'ner du, hört dich des Volkes
Ohr!
(*Sie drängen Friedrich bei Seite. Edel-
knaben treten auf.*)

VIER EDELKNABEN

Macht Platz für Elsa, unsere Frau:
Die will in Gott zum Münster geh'n.
(*Ein langer Zug von Frauen in reichen
Gewändern schreitet aus der Kem-
enate dem Münster zu.*)

MÄNNER UND FRAUEN

Gesegnet soll sie schreiten,
Die lang' in Demut litt;
Gott möge sie geleiten,
Gott hüte ihren Schritt!
Sie naht, die Engelgleiche,
Von keuscher Glut entbrannt!
Heil dir, o Tugendreiche!
Heil Elsa von Brabant!
(*Elsa ist im Zuge aufgetreten; Ortrud
folgt.*)

ORTRUD

Zurück, Elsa! Nicht länger will ich dul-
den,
Dass ich gleich einer Magd dir folgen
soll!
Den Vortritt sollst du überall mir
schulden,
Vor mir dich beugen sollst du demut-
voll!

MÄNNER UND FRAUEN

Was will das Weib?

ELSA

Um Gott! Was muss ich sehn?
Welch jäher Wechsel ist mit dir ge-
'scheh'n?

ORTRUD

Weil eine Stund' ich meines Wert's ver-
gessen,

Glaubest du, ich müsste dir nur krie-
chend nah'n?
Mein Leid zu rächen will ich mich ver-
messen,
Was mir gebührt, das will ich nun
empfah'n.

ELSA

Weh! lies ich durch dein Heucheln
mich verleiten,
Die diese Nacht sich jammernd zu mir
stahl:
Wie willst du nun in Hochmut vor mir
schreiten,
Du, eines gottgerichteten Gemahl!

ORTRUD

Wenn falsch Gericht mir den Gemahl
verbannte,
War doch sein Nam' im Lande hochge-
ehrt;
Als aller Tugend Preis man ihn nur
nannte,
Gekannt, gefürchtet war sein tapfres
Schwert.
Der deine, sag', wer sollte hier ihn ken-
nen,
Vermagst du selbst den Namen nicht zu
nennen!

MÄNNER UND FRAUEN

Was sagt sie? Ha! was tut sie kund?
Sie lästert! Wehret ihrem Mund!

ORTRUD

Kannst du ihn nennen, kannst du uns
es sagen,
Ob sein Geschlecht, sein Adel wohl be-
währt?
Woher die Fluten ihn zu dir getragen,
Wann und wohin er wieder von dir
fährt?
Ha, nein! Wohl brächte ihm es schlim-
me Not,
Der kluge Held die Frage drum verbot!

MÄNNER UND FRAUEN

Ha! spricht sie wahr? Welch' schwere
Klagen!
Sie schmähet ihn! Darf sie es wagen?

ELSA

Du Lästerin! Ruchlose Frau!
Hör', ob ich Antwort mir getrau'!
So rein und edel ist sein Wesen,
So tugendreich der hehre Mann,
Dass nie des Unheils soll genesen,
Wer seiner Sendung zweifeln kann!

MÄNNER

Gewiss! Gewiss!

THE FOUR NOBLES

Ha! Who are you? Frederick! Is it
    true?
You dare be here, a prey to every
    knave!

FREDERICK

You soon will see how far my daring
    takes me,
Quite soon your eyes will see it plain
    as daylight!
He who so boldly calls you forth to war
I will accuse of treachery to God!

THE FOUR NOBLES

What say you? Blusterer! What will
    you do?
You maniac, don't let the people hear!

(*They pull Frederick aside. Four pages
    appear.*)

PAGES

Make way, make way, our Lady Elsa
    comes!
Upheld by God she passes by!

*A long train of ladies, richly clad, ad-
vances from the Kemenate towards
the Minster.*

NOBLES AND RETAINERS

Most blessed be the pathway
Of her who long bore woe.
May God direct her footsteps
And ever guide her so!
She comes, so like an angel!
A heavenly habitant!
All hail, most rich in virtue
Hail, Elsa of Brabant!

(*Elsa has advanced in the procession.
Among the last ladies who follow her
is Ortrud.*)

ORTRUD

Stand back, Elsa! No longer will I bear
Being but a serving maid to follow you!
The precedence is mine, and you must
    yield it!
Before me you will humbly bow your
    head!

PAGES AND RETAINERS

What does she want?

ELSA

Great Heaven! What must I see?
What sudden change has taken place in
    you?

ORTRUD

Though I had let my worth to be
    forgotten

Do you think that I should crawl
    before your feet?
My woes and sufferings cry aloud for
    vengeance!
That which is due, that will I now
    receive!

ELSA

Woe! Have I let your feigning words
    mislead me,
Who just last night stole wailing to my
    door?
How dare you now so proudly step
    before me,
You, spouse of him the Lord of all
    has judged?

ORTRUD

When truthless judgment made my
    spouse an outlaw,
His was a name most honored in the
    land.
Men held him as a paragon of virtue,
Both known and dreaded was his
    valiant sword.
Your husband, though, who is there
here that knows him?
And as for you, you cannot even name
    him!

MEN AND WOMEN

What says she? Ha! What does she tell?
That slanderer! Make her hold her
    tongue!

ORTRUD

Say, can you name him? Can you talk
    about him,
Tell of his race, or of his birth or rank?
Whence did the waters bear him to
    our country?
When will he part from you and sail
    again?
Ah, no! Well might there be a weighty
    cause
Your wily knight holds questioning
    forbid!

MEN AND WOMEN

Ha! Is this true? Her words are
    grievous!
She shames the knight, how dare she do
    it?

ELSA

You slanderer! Woman of lies!
Hear whether I can answer true!
So pure and noble is his nature,
So virtue-rich this gentle man,
That never wretch shall be forgiven
Who doubts that God has sent him
    here!

ELSA

Hat nicht durch Gott im Kampf ge-
schlagen
Mein teurer Held den Gatten dein?
Nun sollt nach Recht ihr alle sagen,
Wer kann da nur der Reine sein?

MÄNNER UND FRAUEN

Nur er! Nur er! Dein Held allein!

ORTRUD

Ha! diese Reine deines Helden,
Wie wäre sie so bald getrübt,
Müsst' er des Zaubers Wesen melden,
Durch den hier solche Macht er übt!
Wagst du ihn nicht darum zu fragen,
So glauben alle wir mit Recht,
Du müssest selbst in Sorge zagen,
Um seine Reine steh' es schlecht!

DIE FRAUEN

Helft ihr vor der Verruchten Hass!

MÄNNER

Macht Platz! Macht Platz! Der König
naht!

(*Der König, Lohengrin, die sächsischen
und brabantischen Grafen und Edlen
sind aus dem Palas herausgeschrit-
ten.*)

DIE MÄNNER

Heil! Heil dem König!
Heil dem Schützer von Brabant!

KÖNIG

Was für ein Streit?

ELSA

Mein Herr! O mein Gebieter!

LOHENGRIN

Was ist?

KÖNIG

Wer wagt es hier den Kirchengang zu
stören?

DES KÖNIGS GEFOLGE

Welcher Streit, den wir vernahmen?

LOHENGRIN

Was seh' ich! Das unsel'ge Weib bei
dir?

ELSA

Mein Retter! Schütze mich vor dieser
Frau!
Schilt mich, wenn ich dir ungehorsam
war!
In Jammer sah ich sie vor dieser Pforte,
Aus ihrer Not nahm ich sie bei mir auf:
Nun sieh', wie furchtbar sie mir lohnt
die Güte,
Sie schilt mich, dass ich dir zu sehr
vertrau'!

LOHENGRIN

Du fürchterliches Weib, steh' ab von
ihr!
Hier wird dir nimmer Sieg! Sag', Elsa,
mir!
Vermocht' ihr Gift sie in dein Herz zu
giessen?
(*Elsa birgt weinend ihr Gesicht an
seiner Brust.*)
Komm! lass in Freude dort diese
Tränen fliessen!

FRIEDRICH

(*tritt auf die Treppe des Münsters*)
O König! Trugbetörte Fürsten! Haltet
ein!

DIE MÄNNER

Was will der hier? Verfluchter, weich'
von dannen!

KÖNIG

Wag'st du zu trotzen meinem Zorn?

FRIEDRICH

O hört mich an!

DIE MÄNNER

Hinweg! Du bist des Todes, Mann!

FRIEDRICH

Hört mich, dem grimmes Unrecht ihr
getan!

KÖNIG

Hinweg!

FRIEDRICH

Gottes Gericht, es ward entehrt,
betrogen!
Durch eines Zaub'rers List seid ihr be-
logen!

DIE MÄNNER

Greift den Verruchten! Hört! Er
lästert Gott!

MEN

Indeed! Indeed!

ELSA

Did not through God my hero conquer
Your husband on the field of arms?
Now shall you all in truth affirm it,
Who stands alone in purity?

MEN AND WOMEN

We know! We know! Your knight
alone!

ORTRUD

Ha! All this purity of your hero,
I fear it would be soon disturbed
If he confessed that magic practice
Through which deeds of such might
were done!
Are you afraid to put the question?
If so, we all are right to think
That you are faced with some mis-
givings
His honor stands in parlous case!

THE WOMEN

Shield her from the accursed one's
hate!

MEN

Make way! Make way! Here comes
the king!

(*The King, Lohengrin, the Saxon and
Brabant nobles advance from the
Palas. Lohengrin and the King press
to the foreground.*)

MEN

Hail, hail, my sovereign!
Hail the Guardian of Barbant!

KING

What is this strife?

ELSA

My Lord, O my defender!

LOHENGRIN

What is't?

KING

Who dares to clamor here before the
Minster?

KING'S ATTENDANTS

What's this strife that we are hearing?

LOHENGRIN

What is this? This unhallowed one with
you?

ELSA

My champion! Shelter me against her
wrath!
Blame me if I have disobeyed your
word!
I saw her weeping here beside the
portal,
And took her to me in her dire distress.
Now see, how harshly she repays my
goodness,
She taunts me for my steadfast faith in
you!

LOHENGRIN

O woman most accursed, away from
her!
Here you can never win!
Say, Elsa, say
If she has poured her poison in your
bosom.
(*She hides her weeping face on his
breast. Lohengrin raises her and
points to the Minster.*)
Come, let us go, and there let your
tears be joyful!

FREDERICK

(*comes foward on the steps of the
Minster*)

O sovereign! Fraud-deluded princes!
Hold a while!

MEN

What does he want? Accursed! Leave
our presence!

KING

How do you dare to brave my wrath?

FREDERICK

Oh, hear me out!

MEN

Away! You are a man condemned!

FREDERICK

Hear me, to whom you've done a
frightful wrong!

THE KING

Away!

FREDERICK

Judgment of God has been betrayed by
falsehood,
A falsehood spun by black sorcerer's
magic!

THE MEN

Seize the accursed one! Hear, he
blasphemes God!

FRIEDRICH

Den dort im Glanz ich vor mir sehe,
Den klage ich des Zaubers an!
Wie Staub vor Gottes Hauch verwehe
Die Macht, die er durch List gewann!
Wie schlecht ihr des Gerichtes wahrtet,
Das doch die Ehre mir benahm,
Da eine Frag' ihr ihm erspartet
Als er zum Gotteskampfe kam!
Die Frage nun sollt ihr nicht wehren,
Dass sie ihm jetzt von mir gestellt:
Nach Namen, Stand und Ehren
Frag' ich ihn laut vor aller Welt!
Wer ist er, der an's Land geschwom-
men,
Gezogen von einem wilden Schwan?
Wem solche Zaubertiere frommen,
Des Reinheit achte ich für Wahn!
Nun soll der Klag' er Rede steh'n:
Vermag er's, so geschah mir recht,
Wo nicht, so sollet ihr erseh'n,
Um seine Reine steh' es schlecht!

DER KÖNIG UND DIE MÄNNER

Welch harte Klagen! Was wird er entgegnen?

LOHENGRIN

Nicht dir, der so vergass der Ehren,
Hab' Not ich Rede hier zu steh'n;
Des Bösen Zweifel darf ich wehren,
Vor ihm wird Reine nie vergeh'n.

FRIEDRICH

Darf ich ihm nicht als würdig gelten,
Dich ruf' ich, König, hoch geehrt;
Wird er auch dich unadlig schelten,
Dass er die Frage dir verwehrt?

LOHENGRIN

Ja, selbst dem König darf ich wehren,
Und aller Fürsten höchstem Rat!
Nicht darf sie Zweifels Last be-
schweren,
Sie sahen meine gute Tat!
Nur Eine ist's, der muss ich Antwort
geben: Elsa!
Elsa! wie seh' ich sie erbeben!
In wildem Brüten muss ich sie ge-
wahren,
Hat sie betört des Hasses Lügenmund?
O Himmel! schirm' ihr Herz vor den
Gefahren!
Nie werde Zweifel dieser Reinen kund!

FRIEDRICH UND ORTRUD

In wildem Brüten darf ich sie ge-
wahren,
Der Zweifel keimt in ihres Herzens
Grund.
Der mir zur Not in dieses Land ge-
fahren,
Er ist besiegt, wird ihm die Frage
kund.

DER KÖNIG UND ALLE MÄNNER

Welch ein Geheimnis muss der Held
bewahren?
Bringt es ihm Not, so wahr' es treu
sein Mund.
Wir schirmen ihn, den Edlen, vor Gefahren;
Durch seine Tat ward uns sein Adel
kund.

ELSA

Was er verbirgt, wohl bräct' es ihm
Gefahren,
Vor aller Welt spräch' es hier aus sein
Mund;
Die er errettet, weh' mir Undankbaren!
Verriet' ich ihn, dass hier es werde
kund.
Wüsst' ich sein Los, ich wollt' es treu
bewahren:
Im Zweifel doch erbebt des Herzens
Grund!

DER KÖNIG

Mein Held! Entgegne kühn dem Ungetreuen!
Du bist zu hehr, um, was er klagt, zu
scheuen!

DIE MÄNNER

Wir steh'n zu dir, es soll uns nicht gereuen!
Dass wir der Helden Preis in dir
erkannt!
Reich' uns die Hand! Wir glauben dir
in Treuen,
Dass hehr dein Nam', auch wenn er
nicht genannt.

LOHENGRIN

Euch Helden soll der Glaube nicht
gereuen,
Werd' euch mein Nam' und Art auch
nie genannt.

FRIEDRICH (zu Elsa)

Vertraue mir! Lass dir ein Mittel
heissen,
Das dir Gewissheit schafft!

ELSA (erschrocken, doch leise)

Hinweg von mir!

FRIEDRICH

Lass mich das kleinste Glied ihm nur
entreissen,
Des Fingers Spitze, und ich schwöre dir,

FREDERICK

This shining knight I see before me,
I here accuse of magic art!
As dust by breath of God is scattered,
So shall his might be blown away!
How badly did you honor judgment
Who took the honor from my name
By sparing but to ask a question
That time he came to join God's
    fight.
The question now shall not be spared
    him,
Which I straightway shall bluntly put:
His station, name and honor
I ask aloud before the world!
Who is he, this most mighty man,
Whom a wild swan has drawn here in
    a boat?
And since he uses magic creatures,
I doubt if he's an honest man!
Now shall he face the charge I make:
If answered, he may prove his cause;
If not, why then it will be plain
His truth and honor look quite bad!

THE KING AND THE MEN

A bitter challenge! How will he make
    an answer?

LOHENGRIN

To you, who have forgot your honor,
I need not deign to make reply.
I disregard the doubts of blackguards,
For such can never soil my name.

FREDERICK

Then, if he holds me too unworthy,
Most noble king, I call on you!
Can he presume you are too lowly,
And so refuse what you may ask?

LOHENGRIN

Yes, even the king I dare not answer,
And all the council of his lords!
Need is there none for them to doubt
    me:
They saw the doughty deed I did!
There's only one to whom I must make
    answer:
Elsa.
Elsa! Why do I see you trembling?
Her heart is torn with dark and fear-
    ful broodings!
Was she deceived by hatred's lying
    mouth?
O heaven! Guard her heart from every
    danger!
Let not suspicion taint this maid so
    pure!

FREDERICK AND ORTRUD

Her breast is torn with dark and fear-
    ful broodings!
A doubt is sprouting in her inmost
    heart!
He will be lost who brought me woe
Within this land, if he but make reply!

THE KING AND MEN

If it's a secret, let the hero keep it.
If he has need, then let him lock his
    lips.
We'll guard him well, this hero, from
    all danger.
His deed revealed that he was nobly
    born!

ELSA

What he conceals might well have
    brought him danger
If it were made known to the world at
    large.
I, whom he rescued, woe, were I un-
    grateful,
Betraying him, by asking for the truth.
But if I knew, I truly would protect it.
(Yet doubt still stirs within my inmost
    heart!)

THE KING

My knight, stand up most boldly to the
    treacher!
You are too true to be afraid of false-
    hood.

THE MEN

We stand by you! And never will we
    rue it,
We see in you a knight of high re-
    nown.
Give us your hand! We hold your
    name in honor!
A name most high, although we know
    it not.

LOHENGRIN

You heroes never shall regret believing,
Although my name and state must stay
    unknown!

FREDERICK (to Elsa)

Just take my word! There is a way of
    knowing
Which will bring certainty!

ELSA

Away from me!

FREDERICK

I'd have the littlest bit of flesh torn
    from him,
A tip of finger, and I swear to you,

Was er dir hehlt, sollst frei du vor dir
sehn,
Dir treu, soll nie er dir von hinnen
gehn.

ELSA

Ha, nimmermehr!

FRIEDRICH

Ich bin dir nah' zur Nacht
Rufst du, ohn' Schaden ist es schnell
vollbracht!

LOHENGRIN

Elsa, mit wem verkehrst du da?
(zu Ortrud und Friedrich)
Zurück von ihr, Verfluchte!
Dass nie mein Auge je
Euch wieder bei ihr seh'!
Elsa, erhebe dich! In deiner Hand,
In deiner Treu' liegt alles Glückes
Pfand!
Lässt nicht des Zweifels Macht dich
ruh'n?
Willst du die Frage an mich tun?

ELSA

Mein Retter, der mir Heil gebracht!
Mein Held, in dem ich muss vergeh'n,
Hoch über alles Zweifels Macht
Soll meine Liebe steh'n!

LOHENGRIN

Heil dir, Elsa! Nun lass vor Gott uns
geh'n!

DIE MÄNNER UND FRAUEN

Seht! seht! Er ist von Gott gesandt!
Heil ihm! Heil Elsa von Brabant!

DRITTER AUFZUG
ERSTE SZENE

*Das Brautgemach; rechts ein Erker-
turm mit offenem Fenster. Musik
hinter der Bühne, der Gesang ist erst
entfernt, dann näher kommend. In
der Mitte des Liedes werden rechts
und links im Hintergrunde Türen
geöffnet: rechts treten die Frauen
auf, welche Elsa,—links die Männer
mit dem König, welche Lohengrin
geleiten; Edelknaben mit Lichtern
voraus.*

MÄNNER UND FRAUEN

Treulich geführt ziehet dahin,
Wo euch der Segen der Liebe
bewahr'!
Siegreicher Mut, Minnegewinn
Eint euch in Treue zum seligsten
Paar.

Streiter der Tugend, schreite voran!
Zierde der Jugend, schreite voran!
Rauschen des Festes seid nun entron-
nen,
Wonne des Herzens sei euch gewon-
nen!
Duftender Raum, zur Liebe ge-
schmückt,
Nehm' euch nun auf, dem Glanze ent-
rückt.
Treulich geführt ziehet nun ein,
Wo euch der Segen der Liebe bewahr'!
Siegreicher Mut, Minne so rein
Eint euch in Treue zum seligsten Paar.

ACHT FRAUEN

Wie Gott euch selig weihte,
Zu Freuden weih'n euch wir;
In Liebesglücks Geleite
Denkt lang der Stunde hier!
(*Die Edelknaben mahnen zum Auf-
bruch. Die Züge ordnen sich wieder,
und während des Folgenden schreiten
sie an den Neuvermählten vorüber,
so dass die Männer rechts, die Frauen
links das Gemach verlassen.*)

CHOR

Treulich bewacht bleibet zurück,
Wo euch der Segen der Liebe bewahr'!
Siegreicher Mut, Minne und Glück
Eint euch in Treue zum seligsten Paar.
Streiter der Tugend, bleibe daheim!
Zierde der Jugend, bleibe daheim!
Rauschen des Festes seid nun entronn-
nen,
Wonne des Herzens sei euch gewonnen!
Duftender Raum, zur Liebe ge-
schmückt,
Nahm euch nun auf, dem Glanze ent-
rückt.
Treulich bewacht bleibet zurück,
Wo euch der Segen der Liebe bewahr'!
Siegreicher Mut, Minne und Glück
Eint euch in Treue zum seligsten Paar.
(*Elsa ist, wie überselig Lohengrin an
die Brust gesunken. Lohengrin setzt
sich, während der Gesang verhallt,
auf einem Ruhebett am Erkerfenster
nieder, indem er Elsa sanft nach sich
zieht.*)

LOHENGRIN

Das süsse Lied verhallt; wir sind allein,
Zum erstenmal allein, seit wir uns
sahn;
Nun sollen wir der Welt entronnen sein,
Kein Lauscher darf des Herzens
Grüssen nahn.
Elsa, mein Weib! Du süsse, reine Braut!
Ob glücklich du, das sei mir nun ver-
traut!

The thing he hides he freely will reveal.
Then, true to you, he'll never leave your side.

ELSA

Ha! Nevermore!

FREDERICK

This night I shall be near.
Call me, no harm, and straight the deed is done!

LOHENGRIN

Elsa, with whom do you converse?
(to Ortrud and Frederick)
Away from her, accursed ones!
And never let my eyes
See you again with her!
Elsa, get up, my love! Within your hand,
Within your trust lies all my pledge of joy!
Let not the power of doubt hold sway.
Is there a question you would risk?

ELSA

My champion, who has saved my life!
My knight, in whom I lose myself!
High over every power of doubt,
Love is the king I own!

LOHENGRIN

Come then, Elsa! Come, in the sight of God!

THE MEN AND WOMEN

See, this man was sent from God!
Hail, knight! Hail, Elsa of Brabant!

ACT THREE

SCENE 1

The bridal chamber. The bridal procession, accompanied by instruments and voices, enters the room. At the right door the ladies enter, leading Elsa; at the left the king and nobles, leading Lohengrin, both being preceded by pages with lights. When they have reached the center the King leads Lohengrin to Elsa.

MEN AND WOMEN

Faithfully led, enter this place,
Where there await you the blessings of love!
Valorous might, radiant grace,
Here are united by heaven above.

Champion of virtue, enter before!
Champion of beauty, enter before!
Sounds of the revels now are forsaken,
Joys of the bridal soon will awaken!
Chamber of love with fragrance about,
Splendor and pomp must now be shut out.
Faithfully led, enter this place,
Where there await you the blessings of love!
Valorous might, radiant grace
Here are united by heaven above!

EIGHT WOMEN

As God has given you blessings,
We joy to bless you too.
In joys to come remember
This bower blest for two!
(*The pages give a signal for departure. The men go off right, the women left, singing as follows:*)

GENERAL CHORUS

Faithfully watched, rest in this place,
Where there await you the blessings of love!
Valorous might, radiant grace,
Now are united by heaven above.
Champion of virtue, here you will stay,
Champion of beauty, here you will stay!
Sounds of the revels now are forsaken,
Joys of the bridal soon will awaken!
Chamber of love, with fragrance about,
Splendor and pomp must now be shut out.
Faithfully watched, rest in this place,
Where there await you the blessings of love!
Valorous might, radiant grace
Now are united by heaven above!
(*Elsa, overcome by emotion, sinks upon Lohengrin's breast. As the music dies away he seats himself on the couch and draws Elsa gently towards him.*)

LOHENGRIN

The blissful song has ceased; we are alone
The first and only time since first we met.
Now have we put the world a world away.
No listener hears the greetings from our hearts.
Elsa, my wife: my sweet, my maiden bride!
And are you happy, now that you are mine?

ELSA

Wie wär ich kalt, mich glücklich nur
　zu nennen,
Besitz' ich aller Himmel Seligkeit!
Fühl' ich zu dir so süss mein Herz ent-
　brennen,
Atme ich Wonnen, die nur Gott ver-
　leiht.

LOHENGRIN

Vermagst du, Holde, glücklich dich
　zu nennen,
Gibst du auch mir des Himmels Selig-
　keit!
Fühl' ich zu dir so süss mein Herz ent-
　brennen,
Atme ich Wonnen, die nur Gott ver-
　leiht!
Wie hehr erkenn' ich uns'rer Liebe We-
　sen!
Die nie sich sah'n, wir hatten uns
　geahnt:
War ich zu deinem Streiter auserlesen,
Hat Liebe mir zu dir den Weg
　gebahnt:
Dein Auge sagte mir dich rein von
　Schuld,
Mich zwang dein Blick zu dienen
　deiner Huld.

ELSA

Doch ich zuvor schon hatte dich
　gesehen,
In sel'gem Traume warst du mir
　genaht;
Als ich nun wachend dich sah vor mir
　stehen,
Erkannt' ich, dass du kamst auf Gottes
　Rat.
Da wollte ich vor deinem Blick zer-
　fliessen,
Gleich einem Bach unwinden deinen
　Schritt,
Gleich einer Blume, duftend auf der
　Wiesen,
Wollt' ich entzückt mich beugen
　deinem Tritt!
Ist dies nur Liebe? Wie soll ich es
　nennen,
Dies Wort, so unaussprechlich wonne-
　voll,
Wie, ach! dein Name, den ich nie soll
　kennen,
Bei dem ich nie mein Höchstes nennen
　soll!

LOHENGRIN

Elsa!

ELSA

Wie süss mein Name deinem Mund ent-
　gleitet!
Gönnst du des deinen holden Klang
　mir nicht?
Nur, wenn zur Liebesstille wir geleitet,
Sollst du gestatten, dass mein Mund
　ihn spricht.
Einsam, wenn niemand wacht;
Nie sei der Welt er zu Gehör gebracht!

(*Lohengrin umfasst Elsa freundlich und
deutet durch das offene Fenster auf
den Blumengarten.*)

LOHENGRIN

Atmest du nicht mit mir die süssen
　Düfte?
O wie so hold berauschen sie den Sinn!
Geheimnisvoll sie nahen durch die
　Lüfte,
Fraglos geb' ihrem Zauber ich mich
　hin.
So ist der Zauber, der mich dir verbun-
　den,
Da als ich zuerst, du Süsse, dich ersah;
Nicht deine Art ich brauchte zu erkun-
　den,
Dich sah mein Aug', mein Herz begriff
　dich da.
Wie mir die Düfte hold den Sinn be-
　rücken,
Nah'n sie mir gleich aus rätselvoller
　Nacht:
So deine Reine musste mich entzücken,
Traf ich dich auch in schwerer Schuld
　Verdacht.

ELSA

Ach, könnt' ich deiner wert erscheinen,
Müsst' ich vor dir nicht bloss vergeh'n,
Könnt' ein Verdienst mich dir vereinen,
Dürft' ich in Pein für dich mich seh'n!
Wie du mich trafst vor schwerer Klage,
O wüsste ich auch dich in Not;
Dass mutvoll ich ein Mühen trage,
Kennt' ich ein Sorgen, das dir droht!
Wär' das Geheimnis so geartet,
Das aller Welt verschweigt dein Mund?
Vielleicht, dass Unheil dich erwartet,
Würd' aller Welt es offen kund?
Wär' es so und dürft' ich's wissen,
Dürft' ich in meiner Macht es seh'n,
Durch keines Droh'n sei mir's entris-
　sen,
Für dich wollt' ich zum Tode geh'n.

ELSA

How cold I'd be to merely say I'm
happy,
When I possess all heaven's blessed-
ness!
Feeling so sweetly how my heart is
glowing,
Raptures I breathe that only God be-
stows!

LOHENGRIN

If you, my fair one, hold yourself for
happy,
Know that you've given me celestial
bliss!
Sweet is the feeling glowing in my
bosom,
Raptures I breathe that only God be-
stows!
How wondrous is the love that now
unites us!
Before we met we had divined that
love.
The choice was made that I should be
your champion,
But love it was that showed the way
to you.
Your eyes informed me you were free
from guilt.
I saw your glance: and knew myself
your knight.

ELSA

Yet let me tell I had already seen you.
You came to me in semblance of a
dream.
I woke and saw you there standing
before me.
I knew then that you came at God's
behest.
Your glance awoke a wish to melt before you
And like a brook to wind about your
path;
Or, like a flower, making meadow
fragrant,
So did I wish to bow beneath your
step.
Is this what love is? How shall I de-
scribe it,
This word, that tells of joy beyond
mere words,
Or like your name, ah, which I may not
utter,
With which I cannot name my highest known?

LOHENGRIN

Elsa!

ELSA

How sweet my name sounds when I
hear you say it!
Why do you grudge the gracious sound
of yours?
Only when love in stillness holds us
closely,
You must allow my mouth to speak
your name.
Stilly, when no one wakes;
Never in hearing of the world outside.

(*Lohengrin tenderly embraces Elsa,
and points through the open case-
ment to the flower garden.*)

LOHENGRIN

Say, do you breathe, as I, the sweet
aroma?
Oh, how its odor ravishes the sense!
Mysteriously it brings to us its frag-
rance;
Questionless do I let its magic bless.
Such is the magic that has bound me
to you,
From that first of days, O sweet one,
when we met.
No need to ask you whence you were
descended:
Eyes knew the truth, and heart did
understand.
And as this fragrance gently takes my
senses,
Wafted to me by enigmatic night,
Even that way your purity enthralled
me,
Though heavy slander tried to hide
your worth.

ELSA

Ah, could I prove that I am worthy,
Not seem like nothing in your eyes!
Could I perform some deed to lift me,
Could I endure some pain for you!
And as you found me crushed with
sorrow,
Could I but save you too from ills!
That bravely I might bear some
burden,
Know of a sorrow threatening you!
Oh, has this secret such a nature
That it must ever seal your lips?
Perhaps disaster would await you,
If you revealed it to the world.
Were it so! And if I knew it,
If I could have it in my power,
No threat on earth could tear it from
me!
For you I'd even go to death!

LOHENGRIN

Geliebte!

ELSA

O mach' mich stolz durch dein Ver-
trauen,
Dass ich in Unwert nicht vergeh'!
Lass dein Geheimnis mich durch-
schauen,
Dass, wer du bist, ich offen seh'!

LOHENGRIN

Ach, schweige, Elsa!

ELSA

Meiner Treue
Enthülle deines Adels Wert!
Woher du kamst, sag' ohne Reue,
Durch mich sei Schweigens Kraft be-
währt!

LOHENGRIN

Höchstes Vertrau'n hast du mir schon
zu danken,
Da deinem Schwur ich Glauben gern
gewährt;
Wirst nimmer du vor dem Gebote wan-
ken,
Hoch über alle Frau'n dünkst du mich
wert!
An meine Brust, du Süsse, Reine!
Sei meines Herzens Glühen nah,
Dass mich dein Auge sanft bescheine,
In dem ich all' mein Glück ersah!
O, gönne mir, dass mit Entzücken
Ich deinen Atem sauge ein!
Lass fest, ach! fest an mich dich
drücken,
Dass ich in dir mög' glücklich sein!
Dein Lieben muss mir hoch entgelten
Für das, was ich um dich verliess;
Kein Los in Gottes weiten Welten
Wohl edler als das meine hiess.
Böt' mir der König seine Krone,
Ich dürfte sie mit Recht verschmähn:
Das Einz'ge, was mein Opfer lohne,
Muss ich in deiner Lieb' ersehn!
Drum wolle stets den Zweifel meiden,
Dein Lieben sei mein stolz Gewähr!
Denn nicht komm' ich aus Nacht und
Leiden,
Aus Glanz und Wonne komm' ich her!

ELSA

Hilf Gott! was muss ich hören!
Welch Zeugnis gab dein Mund!

Du wolltest mich betören,
Nun wird mir Jammer kund!
Das Los, dem du entronnen,
Es war dein höchstes Glück:
Du kamst zu mir aus Wonnen,
Und sehnest dich zurück!
Wie soll ich Ärmste glauben,
Dir g'nüge meine Treu'?
Ein Tag wird dich mir rauben,
Durch deiner Liebe Reu'!

LOHENGRIN

Halt' ein, dich so zu quälen!

ELSA

Was quälest du mich doch!
Soll ich die Tage zählen,
Die du mir bleibest noch?
In Sorg' um dein Verweilen
Verblüht die Wange mir;
Dann wirst du mir enteilen,
Im Elend bleib' ich hier!

LOHENGRIN

Nie soll dein Reiz entschwinden,
Bleibst du von Zweifel rein!

ELSA

Ach, dich an mich zu binden,
Wie sollt' ich mächtig sein?
Voll Zauber ist dein Wesen,
Durch Wunder kamst du her;
Wie sollt' ich da genesen,
Wo fänd ich dein' Gewähr?

(Sie hält an, wie um zu lauschen.)

Hörtest du nichts? Vernahmest du kein
Kommen?

LOHENGRIN

Elsa!

ELSA

Ach nein! Doch dort! Der Schwan, der
Schwan!
Dort kommt er auf der Wasserflut ge-
schwommen,
Du rufest ihm, er zieht herbei den
Kahn!

LOHENGRIN

Elsa! Halt' ein! Beruh'ge deinen Wahn!

ELSA

Nichts kann mir Ruhe geben,
Dem Wahn mich nichts entreisst,
Als, gelt' es auch mein Leben,
Zu wissen, wer du sei'st!

LOHENGRIN

Elsa, was willst du wagen?

LOHENGRIN

Beloved!

ELSA

Oh make me proud by your confiding,
Else I must feel I have no worth.
Open your secret to my honor,
That, who you are, I'll frankly know!

LOHENGRIN

Ah, silence, Elsa!

ELSA

O, my true love
Reveal to me your princely worth!
Without regret say where you came
   from:
Through me let silence' strength be
   proved.

LOHENGRIN

Greatest of trust already has been
   shown you,
For I placed fullest faith upon your
   oath.
If you will never break the oath you
   swore me,
Then of all women you will be the
   peer!
Come to my breast, you sweet and pure
   one!
Be near my glowing, beating heart
That I may feel your eyes' soft
   radiance,
In which I see my happiness!
Oh, grant to me that rarest rapture,
That I may breathe the air you
   breathe.
Cling fast, ah, cling to me so closely,
That I may share your happiness!
Your love must make a high repay-
   ment
For all, which for your sake I lost.
No destiny in God's wide world
Can be nobler than the one that's
   mine!
And even if the crown were offered
I might reject it with good right.
The only thing that can repay me
I look for in your love alone!
Your love shall be my proudest pledge.
So cast aside your doubts forever,
Your love shall be my proudest pledge.
I came not here from night and sor-
   row,
From joy and splendor I have come!

ELSA

O God, what do you tell me!
What's this you have divulged?

You wanted to beguile me,
I know my wretched fate!
The lot that you forsook
Was your highest happiness.
You came to me from joys
And are longing to go back.
How could such wretch as I
Think my love might hold you here?
A day will come that robs me,
When your love is turned to rue!

LOHENGRIN

Forbear all this self-torture!

ELSA

Then do not torture me.
Why should I count the days
That will remain with me?
In dreading your departure
My cheeks will lose their bloom,
And then when off you hasten,
I'm left here in my woe!

LOHENGRIN

Never your charms will lessen
If you stay free from doubt!

ELSA

Ah, how can I bind you to me:
What power do I own?
Your nature is of magic,
And magic brought you here.
What is my fate thereafter,
Where my security?

   (*She starts, and pauses, listening.*)

Did you not hear? Is not that someone coming?

LOHENGRIN

Elsa?

ELSA

Ah, no! It's there, the swan, the swan!
I see him coming on the watery high-
   ways!
You call him here! I see him draw the
   skiff!

LOHENGRIN

Elsa, forbear! And give your fancies
   rest!

ELSA

No, I cannot be peaceful,
And nothing gives them rest,
But—though my life be forfeit—
The knowledge who you are.

LOHENGRIN

Elsa, why do you dare this?

ELSA

Unselig holder Mann,
Hör', was ich dich muss fragen!
Den Namen sag' mir an!

LOHENGRIN

Halt' ein!

ELSA

Woher die Fahrt?

LOHENGRIN

Weh' dir!

ELSA

Wie deine Art?

LOHENGRIN

Weh' uns, was tatest du!
(*Friedrich und die vier brabantischen
Edlen brechen mit gezücktem
Schwerte herein.*)

ELSA

Rette dich! Dein Schwert! Dein
Schwert!
(*Lohengrin streckt Friedrich, da er
nach ihm ausholt, mit einem Streiche
tot zu Boden. Den entsetzten Edlen
entfallen die Schwerter, sie stürzen
zu Lohengrins Füssen auf die Kniee.*)

LOHENGRIN

Weh; nun ist all' unser Glück dahin!

ELSA

Allewiger, erbarm' dich mein!

LOHENGRIN

Tragt den Erschlag'nen vor des
Königs Gericht!
(*Die Edlen nehmen Friedrichs Leiche
auf und entfernen sich mit ihr. Lo-
hengrin läutet an einem Glocken-
zuge: zwei Frauen treten ein.*)
Sie vor den König zu geleiten,
Schmückt Elsa, meine süsse Frau!
Dort will ich Antwort ihr bereiten,
Dass sie des Gatten Art erschau'!
(*Er entfernt sich. Die Frauen geleiten
Elsa ab.*)

LETZTE SZENE

*Als der Vorhang in die Höhe gezogen
wird, stellt die Bühne wieder die Aue
am Ufer der Schelde, wie im ersten
Aufzuge, dar. Von verschiedenen
Seiten gelangt nach und nach der
brabantische Heerbann auf die Scene.
Als die Brabanter alle eingetroffen
sind, zieht König Heinrich mit seinem Heerbann ein.*

DIE BRABANTER

Heil, König Heinrich!
König Heinrich Heil!

DER KÖNIG

Habt Dank, ihr Lieben von Brabant!
Wie fühl' ich froh mein Herz entbrannt,
Find' ich in jedem deutschen Land
So kräftig reichen Heerverband!
Nun soll des Reiches Feind sich nah'n,
Wir wollen tapfer ihn empfahn:
Aus seinem öden Ost daher
Soll er sich nimmer wagen mehr!
Für deutsches Land das deutsche
Schwert!
So sei des Reiches Kraft bewährt!

ALLE MÄNNER

Für deutsches Land has deutsche
Schwert!
So sei des Reiches Kraft bewährt!

KÖNIG

Wo weilt nun der, den Gott gesandt
Zum Ruhm, zur Grösse von Brabant?
(*Die vier brabantischen Edlen bringen
auf einer Bahre Friedrichs verhüllte
Leiche getragen und setzen sie in der
Mitte der Bühne nieder.*)

ALLE

Was bringen die? Was tun sie kund?
Die Mannen sind's des Telramund.

KÖNIG

Wen führt ihr her? Was soll ich
schau'n?
Mich fasst bei eurem Anblick Grau'n!

DIE VIER EDLEN

So will's der Schützer von Brabant:
Wer dieser ist, macht er bekannt.
(*Elsa, mit Gefolge von Frauen, tritt
auf.*)

DIE MÄNNER

Seht Elsa naht, die Tugendreiche!
Wie ist ihr Antlitz trüb' und bleiche!

DER KÖNIG (*geleitet Elsa zu einem Sitz*)
Wie muss ich dich so traurig seh'n?
Will dir so nah' die Trennung geh'n?

STIMMEN

Macht Platz dem Helden von Brabant!
(*Lohengrin ist aufgetreten.*)

KÖNIG

Heil deinem Kommen, teurer Held!
Die du so treulich riefst in's Feld,
Die harren dein in Streites Lust,
Von dir geführt, des Sieg's bewusst.

ELSA

Uncanny, gracious man,
Hear what I now must ask you:
The name you truly bear . . .

LOHENGRIN

Forbear!

ELSA

From whence you came . . .

LOHENGRIN

Woe's you!

ELSA

What is your birth?

LOHENGRIN

Woe's us! What have you done!

(*Frederick and four Brabant nobles
burst in with drawn swords.*)

ELSA

Save yourself! Your sword! Your
sword!

(*She hastily hands the sword to Lohengrin, who quickly draws it and with
one blow strikes Frederick dead. The
four nobles kneel to Lohengrin.*)

LOHENGRIN

Woe! Now the joy that we owned has
fled!

ELSA

All-Merciful, O pity me!

LOHENGRIN

Bear hence the body to the King's judgment hall.

(*The four nobles take up Frederick's
corpse and depart with it. Lohengrin
pulls a bell, and two ladies enter.*)

LOHENGRIN

To lead her into my sovereign
Attire her as my lovely bride.
There will her answer be made ready,
So she may learn her husband's state.

(*Lohengrin leaves sorrowfully.*)

FINAL SCENE

*The plain of the Scheldt is seen, as in
the first act. The Brabant army enters
on both sides, each division being
led by a Count, whose standard
bearer plants his banner in the
ground. Around these banners the
adherents of the various leaders assemble. When all the Brabant force
has arrived, the King enters with the
Saxons and Thuringians.*

ALL THE MEN

Hail, Hail, King Henry!
Hail, King Henry, Hail!

THE KING

Have thanks, good liegemen of Bra-
bant!
Now is my heart aglow with pride!
May I, in every German land
Find such a strong and valiant band!
Now let the kingdom's foe appear,
We'll take him on, we'll meet him here!
Out of his barren Eastern plain
He'll never dare to fight again!
For German land the German sword!
So be our country's land prepared!

THE MEN

For German land the German sword!
Thus be our country's might on guard!

THE KING

Where tarries he, whom God has sent?
For fame and glory of Brabant?

(*The four nobles bring Frederick's cov-
ered body, which they set down.*)

ALL

What do they bring? What do they
want?
The men are those of Telramund.

THE KING

Whom do you bear? What must I see?
Your faces show your news is dread!

THE FOUR NOBLES

So wills the Guardian of Brabant.
The man we bear he'll soon make
known.

(*Elsa, followed by a train of ladies,
advances.*)

THE MEN

Look, Elsa comes, most rich in virtue.
Her countenance is pale and troubled.

THE KING (*leading Elsa to a seat*)

Why must I see you look so sad?
Do you find parting hard to take?

VOICES

Make way, the Guardian of Brabant!
(*Lohengrin enters solemnly.*)

THE KING

Hail to your coming, dearest knight!
Those you so staunchly called to fight,
Wait for you here to give the word
And lead them forth with conquering
sword.

DIE BRABANTER

Wir harren dein in Streites Lust,
Von dir geführt, des Sieg's bewusst.

LOHENGRIN

Mein Herr und König, lass dir melden:
Die ich berief, die kühnen Helden,
Zum Streit sie führen darf ich nicht.

ALLE MÄNNER

Hilf Gott! Welch hartes Wort er
    spricht!

LOHENGRIN

Als Streitgenoss bin nicht ich her-
    gekommen;
Als Kläger sei ich jetzt von euch ver-
    nommen!
(*Er enthüllt Friedrichs Leiche.*)
Zum ersten klage laut ich vor euch
    allen,
Und frag' um Spruch nach Recht und
    Fug:
Da dieser Mann zur nacht mich über-
    fallen,
Sagt, ob ich ihn mit Recht erschlug?

DER KÖNIG UND ALLE MÄNNER

Wie deine Hand ihn schlug auf Erden,
Soll dort ihm Gottes Strafe werden.

LOHENGRIN

Zum and'ren aber sollt ihr Klage hören,
Denn aller Welt nun klag' ich laut,
Dass zum Verrat an mir sich liess be-
    tören
Das Weib, das Gott mir angetraut.

ALLE MÄNNER

Elsa! Wie mochte das gescheh'n!
Wie konntest du dich so vergeh'n?

LOHENGRIN

Ihr hörtet alle, wie sie mir ver-
    sprochen,
Dass nie sie woll' erfragen wer ich bin?
Nun hat sie ihren teuren Schwur ge-
    brochen,
Treulosem Rat gab sie ihr Herz dahin!
Zu lohnen ihres Zweifels wildem
    Fragen
Sei nun die Antwort länger nicht
    gespart:
Des Feindes Drängen durft' ich sie ver-
    sagen,
Nun muss ich künden, wie mein Nam'
    und Art.
Jetzt merket wohl, ob ich den Tag muss
    scheuen:

Vor aller Welt, vor König und vor
    Reich
Enthülle mein Geheimnis ich in
    Treuen!
So hört, ob ich an Adel euch nicht
    gleich!

ALLE MÄNNER UND FRAUEN

Welch Unerhörtes muss ich nun er-
    fahren!
O könnt' er die erzwung'ne Kunde sich
    ersparen!

LOHENGRIN

In fernem Land, unnahbar euren
    Schritten,
Liegt eine Burg, die Monsalvat ge-
    nannt;
Ein lichter Tempel stehet dort in
    mitten,
So kostbar, als auf Erden nichts be-
    kannt;
Drin ein Gefäss von wundertät'gem
    Segen
Wird dort als höchstes Heiligtum be-
    wacht:
Es ward, dass sein der Menschen
    reinste pflegen,
Herab von einer Engelschar gebracht;
Alljährlich naht vom Himmel eine
    Taube,
Um neu zu stärken seine Wunderkraft:
Es heisst der Gral, und selig reinster
    Glaube
Erteilt durch ihn sich seiner Ritter-
    schaft.
Wer nun dem Gral zu dienen ist er-
    koren,
Den rüstet er mit überirdischer Macht;
An dem ist jedes Bösen Trug verloren,
Wenn ihn er sieht, weicht dem des
    Todes Nacht.
Selbst wer von ihm in ferne Land' ent-
    sendet,
Zum Streiter für der Tugend Recht er-
    nannt,
Dem wird nicht seine heil'ge Kraft ent-
    wendet,
Bleibt als sein Ritter dort er uner-
    kannt:
So hehrer Art doch ist des Grales
    Segen,
Enthüllt muss er des Laien Auge
    fliehn;
Des Ritters drum sollt Zweifel ihr nicht
    hegen,
Erkennt ihr ihn, dann muss er von euch
    ziehn.
Nun hört, wie ich verbot'ner Frage
    lohne!

THE BRABANTIANS

We wait for you to give the word,
To lead us forth with conquering
sword.

LOHENGRIN

My lord and sovereign, be enlightened:
They whom I called, these doughty
heroes,—
I dare not summon to the war.

ALL THE MEN

O God! What bitter words to hear!

LOHENGRIN

I have not come to lead you forth to
battle,
But rather am I here as a complain-
ant.
(*He uncovers the corpse.*)
Before you have I come to make my
charges,
And ask for judgment after right.
By night this man attacked and tried
to slay me.
Say, was I right to take his life?

THE KING AND MEN

Just as your earthly hand did smite
him,
So shall God's heavenly hand requite
him.

LOHENGRIN

Now hear another of my charges.
I make complaint to all the world.
My wife has been misled to do me
treason,
That wife which God bestowed on me.

ALL

Elsa! How can this charge be true?
How could you so offend the truth?

LOHENGRIN

You all were present when she gave
her promise
That never would she ask me who I
am.
Now, broken is that sacred oath she
swore to:
Treacherous counsel made her yield
her heart.
To satisfy her prodding wild suspicions
No longer shall that answer be with-
held.
And though I need not heed an urgent
foeman,
Yet must I now reveal my name and
birth.

Now mark me well, if I need fear the
daylight.
Before the world, before the king and
kingdom
I shall now reveal my sacred secret.
So learn if I am princely like as you!

THE MEN AND WOMEN

What wondrous secret must I now be
hearing?
Oh could he be but spared from having
to relate it!

LOHENGRIN

In distant land, no neighbor to your
footsteps,
There is a fastness, Monsalvat by name.
And in its midst there stands a shining
temple,
So costly that the earth knows not its
like.
Therein a blessed, wonder-working
vessel
Is there preserved as holiest of signs.
It was—so purest men might purely
tend it—
Brought down to earth by holy angel
band.
Once every year a dove descends from
heaven
To strengthen it anew with wondrous
power.
It's called the Grail, and faith serene
and blessed
Is shed from it upon the knightly band.
He who is chosen for the Grail's attend-
ance
Is armed therewith with more than
mortal might.
No evil power can ever overthrow him.
To look on the Grail destroys the
dream of death;
And if he's sent to distant regions
When called to be the champion of
right,
Even here will the holy power serve
him.
While he's unknown he's master of the
spell.
Of such high source though is the
blessed vessel,
Revealed, straight will it flee the lay-
man's eye.
And so its knight must never be sus-
pected,
For if once known, then must he leave
the land.
Now hear how I must answer what
was asked me.

Vom Gral ward ich zu euch daher ge-
    sandt;
Mein Vater Parzival trägt seine Krone,
Sein Ritter ich—bin Lohengrin ge-
    nannt.

ALLE MÄNNER UND FRAUEN

Hör' ich so seine höchste Art bewähren,
Entbrennt mein Aug' in heil'gen
    Wonnezähren.

ELSA

Mir schwankt der Boden! Welche
    Nacht!
O Luft, Luft der Unglücksel'gen!
(Sie droht umzusinken; Lohengrin fasst
    sie in seine Arme.)

LOHENGRIN

O, Elsa! Was hast du mir angetan?
Als meine Augen dich zuerst ersah'n,
Zu dir fühlt' ich in Liebe mich
    entbrannt,
Und schnell hatt' ich ein neues Glück
    erkannt:
Die hehre Macht, die Wunder meiner
    Art,
Die Kraft, die mein Geheimnis mir be-
    wahrt,
Wollt' ich dem Dienst des reinsten Her-
    zens weih'n:
Was rissest du nun mein Geheimnis
    ein?
Jetzt muss ich, ach! von dir geschieden
    sein!

KÖNIG, MÄNNER UND FRAUEN

Weh! weh! musst du von uns ziehn,
Du hehrer, gottgesandter Mann!
Soll uns des Himmels Segen fliehn,
Wo fänden dein wir Tröstung dann?

ELSA

Mein Gatte! Nein! ich lass' dich nicht
    von hinnen!
Als Zeuge meiner Busse bleibe hier!
Nicht darfst du meiner bittern Reu'
    entrinnen;
Dass du mich strafest liege ich vor dir!

LOHENGRIN

Ich muss, ich muss, mein süsses Weib!
Schon zürnt der Gral, dass ich ihm
    ferne bleib'!

ELSA

Bist du so göttlich, als ich dich erkannt,
Sei Gottes Gnade n'cht aus dir ver-
    bannt!

Büsst sie in Jammer ihre schwere
    Schuld,
Nicht flieh' die Ärmste deiner Nähe
    Huld!
Verstoss mich nicht, wie gross auch
    mein Verbrechen!
Verlass mich, ach! verlass mich Ärmste
    nicht.

LOHENGRIN

Nur eine Strafe gibt's für dein
    Vergeh'n,
Ach, mich wie dich trifft herbe Pein!
Getrennt, geschieden sollen wir uns
    seh'n:
Dies muss die Strafe, dies die Sühne
    sein!

DER KÖNIG UND DIE EDLEN

O bleib'! O zieh' uns nicht von
    dannen!
Des Führers harren deine Mannen.

LOHENGRIN

O König, hör'! Ich darf dich nicht ge-
    leiten!
Des Grales Ritter, habt ihr ihn erkannt,
Wollt' er in Ungehorsam mit euch strei-
    ten,
Ihm wäre alle Manneskraft entwandt!
Doch, grosser König, lass mich dir weis-
    sagen:
Dir Reinem ist ein grosser Sieg ver-
    liehn!
Nach Deutschland sollen noch in
    fernsten Tagen
Des Ostens Horden siegreich nimmer
    ziehn!

DIE MÄNNER UND FRAUEN

Der Schwan! Der Schwan!
Seht dort ihn wieder nah'n!

ELSA

Entsetzlich! Ha! Der Schwan!
(Man sieht auf dem Flusse den Schwan
    mit dem Nachen anlegen.)

LOHENGRIN

Schon sendet nach dem Säumigen der
    Gral!
(Er tritt zum Ufer und neigt sich zu
    dem Schwan.)
Mein lieber Schwan!
Ach, diese letzte, traur'ge Fahrt,
Wie gern hätt' ich sie dir erspart!
In einem Jahr, wenn deine Zeit
Im Dienst zu Ende sollte geh'n,
Dann, durch des Grales Macht befreit,
Wollt' ich dich anders wiederseh'n!

The holy Grail has sent me here to you.
My father Parsifal rules in my country.
His knight am I, and Lohengrin my
name.

ALL THE MEN AND WOMEN

Just to hark to the lofty tale he tells
us
Has made my scalding eyes pour joyful
teardrops.

ELSA

The floor is reeling! It is night!
Oh, air, air for me most wretched!
(*As she is falling, Lohengrin catches
her in his arms.*)

LOHENGRIN

O, Elsa! What is it you've done to me?
When first my eyes were pleasured by
your sight,
I felt for you a kindling fire of love,
And straightway did a joy uplift my
heart.
The towering might, the wonder of my
state,
The power with which my secret is in-
volved,
These were to serve the purest heart
alive.
Why did you wrest my secret from my
breast?
Now must I—ah!—be parted from
your side!

THE KING, MEN AND WOMEN

Woe! Sorrow! Must you leave our
land,
Most noble man sent here from God?
Must heaven's blessing flee our shores?
Where shall we find our comfort then?

ELSA

My husband! No! I shall not let you
leave me!
To witness my repentance, stay with
me.
You cannot flee my bitter, heart-felt
sorrow.
Punish my error: I am at your feet!

LOHENGRIN

I must, I must, my sweetest wife!
The Grail is wroth that I stay far
away.

ELSA

If you're so godly, as I do believe,
Do not cast off the grace you had from
God.

Let me atone my heavy guilt in tears;
Flee not from her who needs your
saving grace.
Forsake me not, despite my grievous
error.

LOHENGRIN

One sole atonement serves for your
offense.
Ah, I, as you, suffer the bitter hurt.
Cut off, and parted,—this we both must
see.
This is atonement, this is punishment.

THE KING AND MEN

Oh stay, and do not leave us helpless!
Our men are waiting for their leader.

LOHENGRIN

O king, attend! I dare not be their
leader!
The holy servant, if he is but known,
Would, if he broke his vows to help
your battles,
Lose all his godlike, manly strength and
skill.
Yet, mighty monarch, let me make pre-
diction:
You, true-heart, have a victory to
come,
This land of yours shall never feel the
foot-tramp
Of Eastern hordes or now or times
remote.

THE MEN AND WOMEN

The swan! The swan!
Behold, he's drawing near!

ELSA

Oh, horror! Ha! The swan!
(*The swan passes round the front bend
of the stream: he draws the empty
skiff.*)

LOHENGRIN

Too long I've stayed: the Grail has
sent for me.
(*He advances to the bank and bends
over the swan.*)
My trusty swan!
This latest journey pains my heart.
O that it had been spared to you!
Within a year, when time you spent
In service should be at an end,
Freed through the Grail's most holy
power,
I hoped to see you otherwise.
Elsa! Just a year with you, beloved,

O Elsa! Nur ein Jahr an deiner Seite
Hätt' ich als Zeuge deines Glücks er-
sehnt!
Dann kehrte, selig in des Gral's Geleite,
Dein Bruder wieder, den du tot ge-
wähnt.
Kommt er dann heim, wenn ich ihm
fern im Leben,
Dies Horn, dies Schwert, den Ring
sollst du ihm geben:
Dies Horn soll in Gefahr ihm Hilfe
schenken,
In wildem Kampf dies Schwert ihm
Sieg verleiht;
Doch bei dem Ringe soll er mein ge-
denken,
Der einstens dich aus Schmach und
Not befreit!
Leb' wohl! Leb' wohl! Leb' wohl, mein
süsses Weib!
Leb' wohl! Mir zürnt der Gral, wenn
ich noch bleib'!

KÖNIG, MÄNNER UND FRAUEN

Weh! Weh! Du edler, holder Mann!
Welch' harte Not tust du uns an!

ORTRUD (*tritt auf*)

Fahr' heim! Fahr' heim, du stolzer
Helde,
Dass jubelnd ich der Törin melde,
Wer dich gezogen in dem Kahn!
Am Kettlein, das ich um ihn wand,
Ersah ich wohl, wer dieser Schwan:
Es ist der Erbe von Brabant!

ALLE

Ha!

ORTRUD

Dank, dass den Ritter du vertrieben!
Nun gibt der Schwan ihm Heimgeleit!

Der Held, wär' länger er geblieben,
Den Bruder hätt' er auch befreit!

ALLE

Abscheulich Weib! Ha, welch' Ver-
brechen
Hast du in frechem Hohn bekannt!

ORTRUD

Erfahrt, wie sich die Götter rächen,
Von deren Huld ihr euch gewandt!

(*Lohengrin senkt sich, dicht am
Strande, zu einem stummen Gebete
feierlich auf die Kniee. Plötzlich erblickt er eine weisse Taube sich über
den Nachen senken: mit lebhafter
Freude springt er auf und löst dem
Schwane die Kette, worauf dieser sogleich untertaucht: an seiner Stelle
erscheint ein Jüngling — Gottfried.*)

LOHENGRIN

Seht da den Herzog von Brabant,
Zum Führer sei er euch ernannt!

(*Er springt schnell in den Nachen, welchen die Taube an der Kette fasst
und sogleich fortführt.—Gottfried ist
nach vorn geschritten. Alle brabantischen Edlen senken sich vor ihm auf
die Kniee.*)

ELSA

Mein Gatte! Mein Gatte!

(*Sie erblickt Lohengrin bereits in der
Ferne. Sie gleitet in Gottfrieds Armen
entseelt zu Boden.*)

DER VORHANG FÄLLT

Then had I witnessed to your happiness.
You would have joyed to see that one
so blessed
By the Grail, your brother, whom you
fancied dead.
If he comes home when I am living
elsewhere,
This horn, this sword, the ring, give
him in token.
This horn, if he's in danger, brings
protection.
This sword will grant him victory in
arms.
As for the ring, just let it bring
remembrance
Of one who brought you help in time
of need.
Farewell! Farewell! Farewell! My
sweetest wife!
Farewell! Wroth is the Grail if I remain.

THE KING, MEN AND WOMEN

Woe! Woe! Most fair and gracious
man.
What bitter hurt you bring to us!

ORTRUD (*entering foreground*)

Fare home, you haughty hero!
With glee I'll tell that foolish maiden
Who is the one that draws your boat.
I wound that chain about his neck,
And so I recognized your swan.
He is the ruler of Brabant!

ALL

Ha!

ORTRUD

Thanks for the exit of your hero.
Thanks for the exit of the swan.

Your knight, if he had stayed much
longer
Would then have freed your brother
too!

ALL

Accursed witch! Ha, what's the outrage
That you confess in shameless scorn!

ORTRUD

So learn the way the gods take vengeance,
Upon whose grace you turned your
backs!

(*Lohengrin, standing on the bank, now
sinks on his knees in prayer. All eyes
are on him. The white dove of the
Grail flies slowly down. Lohengrin
arises enraptured and takes the chain
from the swan, which sinks. In its
stead appears the youth Gottfried.*)

LOHENGRIN

Behold the ruler of Brabant!
Accept him as your rightful lord!

(*He springs into the boat, which the
dove draws off by the chain. Ortrud
falls with a shriek. Elsa looks with
rapture on her brother, who advances
and makes obeisance to the king. All
the nobles of Brabant kneel before
him. Elsa again looks toward the
river.*)

ELSA

My husband! My husband!

(*Lohengrin is seen in the distance. Elsa,
in Gottfried's arms sinks lifeless to
the ground.*)

CURTAIN